"A rigorous study in dark red. Roc  genealogies of dual Marxist and (it reads its objects of study with a n impulse to lean into the hurt. A in its approach, it serves as a guide for a new necropolitical world in which horror becomes not mere genre, but lived mass experience."

A.V. MARRACCINI, AUTHOR OF *WE THE PARASITES*

"Both elevating the horror genre and invigorating Marxist thinking, *Capitalism: A Horror Story* spells out the urgency of putting our cultural hellscape through a politico-economic sieve. In dialogue with Mark Fisher, Franco Moretti and other illustrious bonesetters of the nightmarish, Greenaway writes with the syncretic precision and utopian zest that have become his trademarks. If you like to scour the depths of the capitalist abyss for signs of hope or simply prefer your political theory served with a side of guts and ghouls, this book is for you."

XAVIER ALDANA REYES, EDITOR OF *HORROR: A LITERARY HISTORY*

"If you've ever wondered why it's now impossible to turn on the TV, walk into a bookshop, or visit the cinema without being assaulted by an array of Gothic monsters this rigorously researched yet enormously readable book is the one to buy. For horror is the zeitgeist of the capitalist age, and the Gothic Marxism posited here not only explains the economic determinants of contemporary culture but also offers a paradoxical light in the darkness. We may all be monsters now — bewildered and broken by forces beyond our control. But in monstrosity new kinds of selves can be imagined and better worlds brought forth."

LINNIE BLAKE, FOUNDER OF THE MANCHESTER CENTRE FOR GOTHIC STUDIES

"Greenaway brilliantly analyzes horror culture and its relationship to the haunted hellscape of contemporary capitalism. The book is full of dazzling horror-related interpretations of Marxist critical theorists as well as incisive close readings of socially relevant cultural works, culminating in an inspiring engagement with the centrality of transgender politics to anti-capitalist critique and utopian futurity. Delivered in rousing, compulsively readable prose, Greenaway's book is an intellectual tour de force, a political manifesto for our moment, and a gothic page-turner. The book's darkly red concluding treatise on monstrous utopianism adds a new riff to Marx's "Theses on Feuerbach": Horror criticism has hitherto only interpreted the world in various ways; the point is to change it."

JOHANNA ISAACSON, AUTHOR OF *STEPFORD DAUGHTERS: WEAPONS FOR FEMINISTS IN CONTEMPORARY HORROR*

"Delves deep into the open maw of our present moment, exploring how the horrors we create offer possibilities for change and fresh modes of resistance. Ever vigilant and informed, Greenaway names our monsters and details the unlikely yet necessary kinship we share with them."

ANDREW F. SULLIVAN, AUTHOR OF *THE MARIGOLD*

"Greenaway convincingly argues for a Gothic Marxism attuned to the fundamentally horrific conditions and effects of contemporary capitalism. In our age of monsters, hope for the future lies in the ruthlessly critical encounter with the monstrous at all levels of culture, and *Capitalism: A Horror Story* is an exemplary study of such a critical theory and practice."

ROBERT T. TALLY JR., AUTHOR OF *THE FICTION OF DREAD: DYSTOPIA, MONSTROSITY, AND APOCALYPSE*

CAPITALISM:
A HORROR STORY

CAPITALISM:
A HORROR STORY

Gothic Marxism and the Dark Side of the Radical Imagination

Jon Greenaway

Published by Repeater Books

An imprint of Watkins Media Ltd

Unit 11 Shepperton House

89-93 Shepperton Road

London

N1 3DF

United Kingdom

www.repeaterbooks.com

A Repeater Books paperback original 2024

1

Distributed in the United States by Random House, Inc., New York.

ISBN: 9781914420887

Ebook ISBN: 9781915672247

Printed and bound in the United Kingdom by TJ Books Limited

This book is dedicated to three people.

To Professor Kate Maxwell, Professor Alana Vincent, and to my comrade, teacher, and mentor, Dr Linnie Blake.

Thank you, all of you.

CONTENTS

INTRODUCTION

A SPECTRE IS
HAUNTING US ALL

It's all true. The bogeyman is real. And you found him.
House of 1,000 Corpses, dir. Rob Zombie (2003)

Let's start with a story. By now it's a familiar one, known for its resonant opening line that has echoed round the world for a hundred and seventy years or more. *A spectre is haunting Europe.* Earlier versions of the opening line of Marx and Engels' *Communist Manifesto* might have translated it as "spook," or even "hobgoblin."

We're being haunted by something…

Capitalism is a horror story. This is the central claim of everything that follows: that behind the apparent rationality and ordered patterns of the world is a mass of violence, and a nightmare of ghosts and hauntings that still lingers on the edge of our collective cultural consciousness. Traditionally, of course, capitalism is seen as strictly a system of economics — one based on wage labour, private property, and profit-motivated production and exchange. Defenders and proponents of this system would be dismissive of any attempt to think of capitalism in anything other than these terms. However, this doesn't seem to address the ways in which the system and ideological structures of capitalism impact us all outside of strictly economic ways, determining social being and even worming its ways into our psyche and our dreams. What's necessary is to think of capitalism less as a system of economic exchange than as a totalising worldview; Nancy Fraser, in *Cannibal Capitalism*, offers an expanded definition well worth quoting in full. Capitalism is

> a societal order that empowers a profit-driven economy to prey on the extra-economic supports it needs to function — wealth expropriated from nature and subject peoples; multiple forms of care work, chronically undervalued when not wholly disavowed; public goods and public powers, which capital both requires and tries to curtail; the energy and creativity of working people. Although they do not appear on corporate balance sheets, these forms of wealth are essential preconditions for the profits and gains that do.[1]

Capitalism doesn't just relate to how things are exchanged but to the more intangible realms of both the imagination and culture. It produces a unique set of effects too — while the ghost story and folkloric monsters predate the industrial capitalism that so concerned Marx, what sets the horrors and hauntings of modernity apart is the fundamental and inescapable idea of alienation. Capitalism alienates human subjects not just from their own work but from one another and from history itself. As a result, history becomes unfamiliar and disorientating, legends and folklore return in strange and unfamiliar new guises, and capitalism itself — apparently stable and natural — is seen as terrifyingly contingent. We are all, at least somewhat, aware of this; after all, at this point the dark side of capitalism is hard to ignore — monsters occupy a central place in the contemporary cultural imagination. Even the politics of the present is full of strange and terrifying transformations and hauntings — the friend/enemy distinction of Schmittian politics allows reactionaries to dehumanise their opponents as monsters. On a more prosaic level, capitalism sees companies in distress as zombies — shambling corpses only fit to be stripped for parts. This is nothing new: Marx, the greatest critic of capitalism, recognised the strange, haunting capacities of capitalism: this system that could take the quotidian and everyday and, through a kind of horrifying alchemy, transform it into a commodity. One famous example is from the opening of the first volume of *Capital*. Think about wood — something natural, mundane, and with a variety of immediate uses, from serving as fuel for your fire to being a material with which to build yourself a table for your home. And yet...

> So soon as it steps forth as a commodity, it is changed into something transcendent. It not only stands with its feet on the ground, but, in relation to all other commodities, it stands on its head, and evolves out of its wooden brain grotesque ideas, far more wonderful than "table turning" ever was.[2]

Enmeshed in the logic of capitalism, the use-value of the natural world is transformed into the occultic possibility of the commodity. When it comes to the horrors of capitalism, these descriptions become graphic examples of body horror. Capitalism is, in Marx's words, sodden with gore — a monster which emerges from the grave dripping with the viscera of those who are chewed to pieces in the gears of the machines. It has to be stated that this is absolutely not just a metaphor. Marx's work — and the work of later Marxists — is full of monsters. Communists have frequently written about vampires, about blood, death, and terror. Capitalism is, in these works, a kind of horror story. You may not agree, but take even the most cursory glimpse at the news, or just out the window, and there are no shortages of horrors that we can identify in our own day and age. Yet to draw attention to it, to use the language of horror and the Gothic, is, for some, a problem; it's often seen as taking Marx's sober and philosophical critique of political economy and undercutting it with a literary penchant for florid and even lurid turns of phrase.[3]

According to this line of criticism, Marx's Gothic metaphors are a kind of aesthetic that can get in the way of the scientific socialism that lies underneath the baggage of his literary and stylistic affectations. However, this writing shouldn't be thought of as just a series of aesthetic choices — as powerful and effective as those aesthetic tools are. Rather, I want to suggest a couple of other ways of reading and understanding this kind of language, and to argue that it is not simply an aesthetic choice that can be discounted in order to get at the "true" philosophical and political content of Marxism; rather, this language not only offers a distinctive philosophical approach to describing the current nightmarish conditions of contemporary capitalism, it also constitutes a theory of history that alters how we consider the past and offers the possibility for a utopian theory of the future.

Firstly, the Gothic and horror rhetoric in Marxism functions as a psychological and phenomenological description of what it feels like, on a personal level, to live through capitalism. Whereas an arid materialism would see the Gothic in culture as a relic — a throwback to the realm of superstition and irrationalism — this only tells us half the story. As is seen in much Marxist writing, from Engels' *Conditions of The Working Classes In England* to so much of Marx's own work, the story of capitalism is fundamentally something that is lived and suffered through. As Mark Steven points out in *Splatter Capital*, Marx's work constantly reiterates the extent to which the processes of capitalism are a kind of body horror, liquefying the flesh and blood of the working classes into commodified labour power.[4] Gothic and horror studies has long argued for understanding the form as a reflection of the cultural anxieties of a given moment. When this kind of cultural history is combined with a Marxist cultural criticism that appreciates horror as a phenomenological element of life under capitalism, this allows us to understand horror and the Gothic not just as disposable entertainment, but as a record of our collective unconsciousness. If we want to know how all the monstrous horror of our time might *feel* — not just on an individual basis but on a social and political one — then understanding both the affective and political power of the Gothic language of Marxism is vital. There is a fine lineage for this kind of thought — I've already mentioned Mark Steven's work, and there is also David McNally's landmark *Monsters of the Market*, a piece of political historiography that traces the Gothic metaphors of Marxism through the political struggles of the nineteenth century all the way to the present.

Academic horror studies, while occasionally suffering from what the V21 Collective refers to as a "naive presentism,"[5] also links horror and the Gothic to the social and political anxieties of a particular moment. If this is the first way of reading the Gothic within Marxism, and of reading horror and the Gothic with Marxism, some may feel that it is a little too impersonal, reducing the psychological complexity of horror to historical correlationism. What is necessary is a way of reading the Gothic and horror with a degree of psychological insight that doesn't sacrifice the political and social elements of a more straightforward Marxist cultural criticism. For this, we can turn to the second strand of "dark Marxism" emerging from the tradition of expressionist European art, French surrealism, and the romantic turn in late-nineteenth-century and early-twentieth-century German philosophical thought. This is the Marxism of Walter Benjamin and the so-called pope of surrealism, André Breton.

For Benjamin, Breton, and the surrealists, Marxism and revolutionary politics collided with their interest in the dreamworld, the irrational, and the political potentialities of the unconscious. The great Marxist critic Walter Benjamin saw the detritus and fragments of culture as profoundly politically meaningful: capitalism's revolution had sought to erase the past — quite literally tearing it down — yet try as it might, it could not eliminate history entirely. Benjamin, the expert navigator of psychogeography, used the figure of the ragpicker to describe his own methodology — the figure on the edge of the tide who examines the flotsam and jetsam washed up and wrecked by the great storm of capitalist progress. In the examination of the past — in Benjamin's case, this took the form of his monumental study of nineteenth-century France — we can see something important about the present that ordinary ("vulgar") Marxism would not be able to articulate. As Benjamin put it in his *Passagen-Werk*, referring to the ruins of the old arcades of Paris, we "believe the charm they exert on us reveals that they still contain materials of vital importance to us — not, of course, for our architecture, the way iron truss-work anticipates our design; but they are vital for our perception, if you will, for the illumination of the situation."[6] In the Gothic remnants of capitalist history, we can see the anxieties and fears of a given cultural moment. Furthermore, this reading of cultural history means that we can see the Gothic as articulating the collective unconscious fears of what it means to live under capitalism at a particular time. This is where, through Gothic Marxism, we can start to construct a Marxist Gothic — a way of reading culture that does not see the Gothic metaphors in Marx or in other cultural objects as just aesthetic decoration, but as a way of diagnosing the psychic toll of capitalism at a particular historical juncture. To put it in Benjamin's words, the Gothic provides an illumination of the situation that other modes of thought cannot.

Both Breton and Benjamin — in their own distinctive ways — sought to deepen and refine Marxist analysis with psychoanalytic ideas borrowed from Freud. Their interest in the dream, the unconscious, and the irrational informed their attempts to bridge a lacunae in Marxist theory, which failed to account for how economic forces and more intangible superstructures, such as art, can interact. Benjamin saw this interaction as a mediation, or a series of meditations, that a good critic could decode and bring into public consciousness. Benjamin criticises Marxist theory as being now swaggering, now scholastic, and instead calls for a Marxism that is alert to the impact of the past upon the present. Rather than try to come up with a comprehensive theory of base/superstructure interaction, it is perhaps better to focus instead on the idea of mediation.

While Benjamin's work places a huge amount of emphasis on the role and centrality of the critic, or the person who can awaken the world to the dream of itself, the role of mediation as essential to consciousness is well established. The great Ernst Fischer, in his landmark book *The Necessity of Art*, built on the work of Engels' Marxist anthropology by arguing that art is almost as old as man and that, by making, by creating, we can mediate the relationship between the self and the world. Creativity, Fischer claimed, is a form of magic, making a symbolic register that becomes — eventually — commodified into art.[7] This historical sense of mediation is the ground from which we can construct the notion of a cultural unconscious (and it provided the reasoning that thinkers such as Breton employed, as was expressed through his art and literary work). Thus, this tradition of thought reinforces the more historicist criticism of the Gothic that I outlined above, with the historical forces of capitalism meeting the psychological experience of having to live through it all.

So, the next question might be: What does Gothic Marxism offer to political thinking and practice that is distinctive? Firstly, it offers an attention to history that does not reduce historical processes to a static totality, but accepts their contingency, flux, and instability. Lukács was famously sceptical of experimental or modern art precisely because it lacked an idea of historical totality, preferring instead mimetic and realist art (particularly novels) in contrast to Bloch, Benjamin, and the French surrealists, who favoured the visual, particular, and fragmentary (which reflected the fragmentary and contingent nature of modernity itself). Secondly, Gothic Marxism offers the possibility of understanding history as something that can change — violently rupture, even. This necessarily requires a dialectical relationship to history and historical processes more generally. Like Gramsci, Benjamin was deeply pessimistic about history, but he also retained a revolutionary optimism of the will. Once more, given the historical context, this is not a surprise — with the rise of fascism, it seemed that whatever hope there was had to be thought of in generational terms, as the Reich was planning for a thousand-year reign. Think of the horrifying Gothic apocalypticism of Brecht, eerily prophetic of the yet-to-arrive nuclear age: "They're planning for thirty thousand years ahead… They're out to destroy everything. Every living cell contracts under their blows… They cripple the baby in the mother's womb."[8] At the same time, Benjamin was writing his lauded theses on history: "The only writer of history with the gift of setting alight the sparks of hope in the past, is the one who is convinced of this: that not even the dead will be safe from the enemy, if he is victorious. And this enemy has not ceased to be victorious."[9] As Stanley Mitchell puts it, "The battles of the past had to be fought and re-fought for if they are not, they may be lost once more."[10] In terms of cultural forms, the Gothic, which focuses on the return of the violence of the past in the present, is an incredible expression of what Benjamin was writing about. Thus, Gothic horror is not just something that is designed to express the fears and anxieties of a capitalist present, focused through the collective social unconscious; it also raises the spectre of possibility — of a better world that can confront the violence, ghosts, and monsters of its past. To put this in slightly more formal terms, the language of the Gothic has a double function: expressing the dialectical possibility of the re-evaluation of the past, and thus the recuperation of the future.

In short, Gothic Marxism is an implementation and cultural expression of Walter Benjamin's "dialectical image," which has direct and immediate political valence. In the mammoth ruins of Benjamin's *Arcades Project*, there's a section entitled "Theory of Knowledge, Theory of Progress," in which Benjamin outlines this idea (developed in conversation with Adorno). Quoting at length helps draw out Benjamin's point:

> It's not that what is past casts its light on what is present, or what is present its light on what is past; rather, image is that wherein what has been comes together in a flash with the now to form a constellation. In other words, image is dialectics at a standstill. For while the relation of the present to the past is a purely temporal, continuous one, the relation of what-has-been to the now is dialectical: is not progression but suddenly emergent. Only dialectical images are genuine images (that is, not archaic).[11]

The Gothic is history out of time, the ghosts and violence of the past becoming visible again in the present. As Anthony Auerbach writes, Benjamin's thought "solicits the imagination,"[12] and it is Benjamin's interest in the way the images of the past can be imaginatively generative for us in the present that is of crucial importance. This understanding of the Gothic and horrifying revenant within capitalism and culture is not just an adopted style (and depoliticising the question of a style or a structure of feeling is a mistake). Rather, Benjamin pointed out — as many other Marxists have too — that the past has unexhausted political potential within it. What if actualising that potential was not the reserve of the critic, but was something that could be performed by all people? What if that potential can be found in even the lowest forms of culture? Enzo Traverso points out that revolutions are about this movement of recuperating the past in all of its Gothic incompleteness, with the aim of catapulting a revolutionary mass toward the future.[13] To comprehend our contemporary experiences as horror is not just to find new ways of articulating our experiences in the present; it is, inevitably, to reorientate our relationship to the past, and even to (re)open the question of the future. It's a startling thought that in the ghosts, monsters, and ruined castles of horror films and Gothic novels there is a reminder that history itself is incomplete — that for all capitalism's attempts to foreclose the present and the future, we still see in our dreams and nightmares the enchanting, terrifying possibility that the world could be otherwise. This possibility haunts capitalism — and those of us who live within it. As the famous line from William Faulkner puts it, "The past is never dead. It's not even past" — all there is is the brutal accumulation of an ever-expanding present. Given these two ways of reading the Gothic within Marxism and the Marxist within the Gothic, what is needed is a theory of culture, history, and revolutionary politics that can articulate the nightmares of capitalism not simply as something monstrous but as a horror that can *end*.

Here then, Gothic Marxism finds its theoretical and philosophical counterpoint in the work of heterodox Marxist and atheist theologian Ernst Bloch. Of particular importance for understanding and refining the theoretical coherence of Gothic Marxism is Bloch's understanding of the non-synchronic. As Bloch put it, we do not all live in the same "Now." Try as it might, capitalism's revolution is incomplete — in a sense, this is a development of other Marxist thought on the combined and uneven development of capitalism, but Bloch recognised that this condition of non-synchronicity was both systemic and existentially personal. This is a profoundly Gothic category, shattering history out of its smooth and easy teleology, forcing us to reckon with our pasts as we struggle to build the future.

This book, then, is about outlining and understanding the ways in which the leftist imagination needs to take into account the Gothic and horrifying in culture and capitalism more generally. However, the complexities of a Gothic Marxism/Marxist Gothic mean that the analysis here can only begin that outline. What Gothic Marxism and a Marxist Gothic allow is both a theoretical investigation of the specificity and genealogy of Gothic Marxism and a diagnostic investigation of the contemporary cultural landscape. As a result, this book moves between a theoretical analysis of the tradition of Gothic Marxism and readings of texts that offer a kind of Marxist Gothic. The majority of the theoretical work is in the opening half. Beginning with an exploration of Ernst Bloch's Marxist philosophy, the opening chapter makes an argument for the "dark way" of being red — a Gothic Marxism not just fit for the historical Gothic but for a continuation of the broader traditions of romantic anti-capitalism. From there, the book moves to some broader historical context regarding the Marxist Gothic, covering the social function of the monster throughout history. Moving on from that, the book draws on Paul Preciado's lecture/polemic to ask: Can the monster speak? And what does it mean to *be* a monster under patriarchal capitalism (reading this polemic alongside films like *Suspiria* and *The VVitch*)? From there the book covers the contemporary gothicism of the internet, a technological haunting that remakes subjectivity. As the book concludes, I offer some arguments about what it would mean to understand utopia as monstrous, and the utopian subject as a monster. So many of us are made into monsters by capitalism, but the monster is the sign that both warns us away from and simultaneously points us toward something new.

On a personal note, I wrote this book out of a deep-seated conviction that the horror films and novels I love are not just sources of pain or revulsion but of *hope* — hard won, contingent, fragile, but still ever present, haunting the wreckage of our shared social and cultural consciousness. Horror *can* end, the world *can* be different, and even the monster might find a new kind of existence. I find hope in horror, and I'm sure I'm not alone in that. It is not an easy or passive optimism — quite the opposite in fact, underscoring that hope is something so often pulled out of blood, pain, terror, and the very darkest moments of our shared existence. As the great Fredric Jameson puts it, "To maintain that everything is a figure of Hope is to offer an analytical tool for detecting the presence of some Utopian content even within the most degraded and degrading cultural product."[14] There is, even here — even in the grimmest darkness, even when facing the most dangerous monster, and even when covered with blood — the possibility of utopia. I invite you to join me in searching for it. After all, as I said right at the beginning, we are haunted by something — and as *The Communist Manifesto* pointed out, what haunts us is the historical embodiment of hope: the spectre of communism.

A Note on "Horror"

There will be a range of texts discussed in the course of this book — many of them recognisably horror films, and perhaps some that readers might be surprised to see included. Though I prefer to avoid getting stuck with an overly narrow genre definition of what we mean by horror and getting bogged down into the morass of taxonomic slapfighting, a brief point of clarification of what exactly is meant by horror might be useful.

The Gothic and horror are closely related, but they should by no means be used interchangeably. As Steven Shapiro and Mark Storey point out, the Gothic is an older, historical form — one which deals with the return of the past into the present and extreme psychological states. Unsurprisingly, the most obvious candidate here would be the ghost story. In contrast, they point out that horror is much more immediate and more rooted in the present tense. They borrow an aphorism from Fredric Jameson, who said that history is what hurts. As they put it, "Horror is the genre above all others that pushes beyond the hurt to the open wound. Horror is what bleeds."[15]

This sense of horror being what bleeds allows for an understanding of the genre that acknowledges some definitional ambiguity, as well as the historical connection horror shares with the Gothic. In a sense, horror is about the literalisation of our current condition, a metaphor made real, and so lends itself extremely well to exploring the political anxieties of capitalism. Aside from its aesthetic markers, there is an affective element to it — as my co-host and I say on *Horror Vanguard*, "Horror wants to do things to your body" — a position which multiple affect theorists have given a more rigorous and thought-out explanation of.[16] (And of course, this directly connects horror with the other forms that seek this kind of affective impact — the biggest two being comedy and erotica). We recognise horror by the way it makes us feel, even if the various generic markers, tropes, and styles might shift. This is why horror hybridises into other forms so well — *Alien* (1979) and *Event Horizon* (1997) are, in terms of affective impact, horror films, despite the science-fictional forms and tropes they use.

The novelist Susanna Clarke, in an Interview published in the *New Yorker*, offers another interesting way of understanding horror. Horror, she says, is predicated upon there being a secret at the heart of the world, on the idea that beneath the appearance of normality lies an obfuscated truth.[17] The point here is not to bring things back to genre distinction or to some idea of a central underlying concept, but rather to focus on the idea — which Clarke phrases in theological terms — of what horror can reveal or obscure. In a way, it is important to reckon with the theological implications of revelation. Our response to truth generally comprises a vacillation between our attraction to it and repulsion from it. But if we see the truth beneath the appearance of things, we can also recognise that neither truth nor surface appearances are immutable, and that — though horrifying and repulsive it might be — genuine change is a real possibility.

CHAPTER ONE

THE DARK WAY OF BEING RED

In 1938, there was a series of debates between European intellectuals that played out in the pages of some short-lived journals of theoretical writing and philosophy. It was a debate around an emergent artistic form — expressionism (in the modern day often eclipsed by its far more famous sibling surrealism). Expressionism was a moment of revolt against a stifling artistic realism and celebrated the subjective rebellion of the individual against a rationalised world that was increasingly restrictive. Artists like Edvard Munch, Paul Klee, and Egon Schiele are perhaps some of the most enduring names and for a time, their work and the work of other expressionists was catalytic in reshaping how European art was considered. For some on the revolutionary left, artistic expressionism, across literature, poetry, and painting, represented a tremendous opportunity for the creation of a genuinely socialist art. On the other side of the debate were not simply traditionalists or reactionaries (though, make no mistake, there were plenty of those too) but rather other socialists. Where one side saw the potential in the expressionist move toward the irrational, the subjective, and the dreamlike, other socialists saw it as forsaking a profound artistic responsibility to engage with the totality of a given social and historical formation. For these socialists, the celebration of expressionism was an abnegation of the political responsibility of the artist and a slide backward into art that could say nothing to the world at large, celebrating a kind of naive and primitive mode of expression that would be left behind in the inferno of capitalist development.

The debate reached its apotheosis in the often fiery polemic exchanges between the German philosopher Ernst Bloch and the Hungarian communist and philosopher György Lukacs. For Bloch, the rise of expressionism was a move in culture that socialists should not ignore — it was the dawning of a new kind of cultural expression and necessarily reflected wider changes and fractures in the social totality that old forms sought to unify into a coherent artistic whole. As a result, expressionism offered resources for an engagement with working-class struggle and subjective interiority that old models of realism were simply unable to address. For Lukacs this was nonsense — an undialectical rejection of actual aesthetic principles and a move that ignored the power and capacity of realism to connect a specifically working-class experience to the whole society in which its class struggle was situated. At best, for someone like Lukacs, expressionist art was subjective indulgence, and at worst it was politically irresponsible.

The debate between the two was fierce — and at times, deeply personal. The two had been intensely close throughout the earliest part of their careers, meeting as young students in Germany, both of them driven by an interest in romanticism and German idealist philosophy. The two began to drift apart thanks to Bloch's interest in religion (which included his writing an excellent book on the German Reformation figure Thomas Munzter as a proto-communist) and Lukacs's own move toward a more orthodox party-line Marxism. For Lukacs, Bloch had wandered from the true path, drifting into non-materialist speculation, unorthodox Hegelianism, and religious — even Messianic — Utopianism. Where Lukacs had become a party philosopher, even becoming directly involved in the Hungarian Communist government, Bloch continued to remain outside of the European Marxist-Leninist movement — being far more heterodox, although always militant, in his commitment.

Reading through their exchange, the sense the reader is left with is of Bloch desperately trying to pull his punches against a friend, whereas Lukacs delivers a masterclass in Marxist polemic. It was left to Bloch's friend Bertolt Brecht to actually respond in kind to Lukacs's invective.[1] Rather than relitigate the debate here, it's worth using the debate to illustrate a divide in Marxist theory that remained central to Bloch's later work — the split between the warm and cold streams of Marxist thought and practice. Bloch is an interesting figure, and it's worth spending a little time fleshing out his argument. In his mammoth and (sadly) still little-read magnum opus *The Principle of Hope*, he undertakes a genuinely astonishingly ambitious mission — to provide an encyclopedic account of hope's persistence through history and, at the same time, to offer a philosophical justification for hope as grounded in materialist reason and as catalytic for political or revolutionary struggle and the possibility of a utopian future. Unsurprisingly, given the scale of the task and Bloch's own florid, loquacious, and expressionist prose style, the book runs to over twelve hundred pages and three volumes in its English translation. Some way into the first, Bloch introduces his distinction between the cold and warm streams of Marxist thought — what he terms the "coldness and warmth of concrete anticipation." They are both equally valid and important modes of thought and political organisation. As Bloch puts it:

> These two ways of being red always go together of course, yet they are distinct from each other. They are related to one another like that which cannot be deceived and that which cannot be disappointed, like acerbity and belief, each in its place and each employed towards the same goal.[2]

So what are these two ways of being red? For Bloch, revolution and the bringing into being of utopia was about the horizon of possibility. The warm stream is a tradition of thought that concerns itself with liberation. As he rather poetically puts it, it is a historical tradition on the side of the poor and the oppressed concerned with "liberating intention and materialistically humane, humanely materialistic real tendency, toward whose goal all these disenchantments are undertaken. From here the strong appeal to the debased, enslaved, abandoned, belittled human being, from here the appeal to the proletariat as the turntable towards emancipation."[3]

For Bloch, culture and history were indelibly marked by this tradition — from the philosophy of Aristotle to the peasant wars of Reformation Europe. This is the Marxism and revolutionary politics of prophetic religious movements, dreamers, and visionaries, seeing revolution as a religious and imaginative act of creatively remaking the world. However, Bloch pointed out that the warm stream alone is insufficient — if revolution is merely concern for emancipation, it would lead to Jacobinism, a utopian excess that would result in the worst kind of retributive violence. As

Bloch puts it, lead needs to be poured into the shoes of this utopian dreaming in order to keep it grounded — and for this one needs the cold stream of Marxism. This is the Marxism of scientific socialism — an unmasking of ideologies and a disenchantment of metaphysical illusion. The split between Lukacs and Bloch maps easily enough onto the two sides of this paradigm, with Bloch as the prophetic figure striding into new territory, and Lukacs as the exemplary figure of the cold stream of Marxism. However, we shouldn't see this in simplistic terms — Bloch, the utopian dreamer, was silent for far too long on the Stalinist purges, and while Lukacs is often seen as a strict Stalinist, his early works are beautiful exemplifications of utopian and Romantic thought. The cold and warm streams are thus not simple or straightforward taxonomies, but we might term them tendencies within thought, philosophy, and historical materialism. Importantly, Bloch emphasises in his own work that these two positions are not antithetical or opposed but dialectically interrelated and profoundly codependent. If the warm stream of prophetic liberation needs the cold stream to maintain a sober sense of judgment, then an overly mechanistic, "cold" Marxism alone would be equally disastrous. As Bloch puts it, such a Marxism avoids

the mists of fanaticism only in as far as it gets bogged down in the swamp of philistinism, of compromise, and finally of betrayal. Only coldness and warmth of concrete anticipation *together* therefore ensure that neither the path in itself nor the goal in itself are held apart from one another dialectically and so become reified and isolated.[4]

What is important is not to ostracise one stream from the

other but to hold both in a productive dialectical tension. Understanding the Gothic in relation to these two tendencies and the wider debate around expressionism allows the cold and warm streams to find a unique mode of cultural expression. Horror as a mode of cultural production has a unique ability to demonstrate in the coldest and most stark material terms the phenomenological experience of capitalism. What are we if not just mere meat to be ground under the gears of this infernal machine that runs on the blood, sweat, and tears of working people all over the world?[5] Within horror you find the most exacting descriptions of our present predicament, stripped of all false optimism and placed before the viewer with an almost cruel lack of sentimentality. On the other hand, the fundamentally unfinished nature of history — the reappearance of the ghost and the supernatural, and the aim of horror to see the world as in some sense (re) enchanted — allows it to mesh well with the warm stream of Marxism. There is a short and simple phrase from Eugene Debs that illustrates this: "The world is not right." The revelation of just how deep and profound that not-rightness *is* is something that horror is uniquely suited to articulating.

We live in the wreckage of what happens under the domination of the cold stream of Marxism — Bloch's warning of philistinism, compromise, and betrayal can only seem eerily prophetic in the wake of the last century of failures and setbacks of mass revolutionary and emancipatory politics in much of the capitalist world. It is a politics that is marked by a dismissive attitude toward the lowest kinds of culture and a suspicion of imagination, and one that sees the ghosts and monsters of history as something to be overcome rather than as making an essential and important point about the fundamental incompleteness and fragmentary nature of our shared existence. However (and thankfully), this is not the only thread of Marxist thought, and rather than subsume the cold stream into sentimentalism and subjectivism, the purpose of a Gothic Marxism is to ground the horror of capitalism in historical materialism, and the same time to treat historical materialism as a living and active force rather than a dictatorial conceit. With this as context then, the argument here is that understanding the Gothic and horrific elements within both Marxism and cultural forms such as film and literature allows for something more than a new understanding of these cultural forms or Marx's literary aesthetics. Rather, what this Gothic Marxist approach allows for is the reviving of a kind of romantic anti-capitalism. What's important in our current moment is for us to collectively put some blood back into an arid and stultifying historical materialism. With this in mind, it's important to construct a philosophical, cultural, and theoretical lineage to ground this notion — the dark way of being red.

The Dark Way of Being Red

There are a number of current genealogies and traditions that examine the intersection of radical politics and the darker sides of the imagination. First comes the historicist tradition of contemporary academic Gothic studies which emerges out of the broader development of cultural studies from thinkers like Richard Hoggart and Raymond Williams. In Gothic studies this has produced some fine scholarship but it can be all too often prone to naive historicism — simply connecting a text to a particular historical event and seeking to do little more than just endlessly describe and preserve the past.[6] While historicism is an essential aspect of cultural studies, the insight that the Gothic and horror express the cultural and social anxieties of a given historical moment is really only the first step, and it does little to engage with how horror is both socially relevant and politically useful in the present moment. The immediate contribution of a more politically engaged kind of cultural criticism is that it allows these cultural products to be more than just the reflection of the conditions under which they were produced.

The dark way of being red is thus formed out of the confluence of several traditions of romantic anti-capitalism: the European Gothic novel of the late eighteenth and nineteenth centuries; German idealist philosophy from Goethe onward (exemplified by Bloch and, in a way, Walter Benjamin); and the artistic and theoretical work of the Freudian-Marxist surrealist movement exemplified by figures like Andre Breton, Max Ernst, and Lenora Carrington. The term "romantic anti-capitalism" was originally coined by Bloch's old friend Lukacs — but Lukacs, like many orthodox Marxists, saw it as essentially and inevitably leading to irrationalism, reactionary politics, and, eventually, fascism.[7] While Lukacs was deeply suspicious of romanticism — for clear and deeply persuasive historical reasons — Michael Löwy and Robert Sayre point out that Lukacs's late writing on Balzac showcases "a much deeper and more subtle analysis… where he stresses that the hatred of the author of the *Comedie Humaine* for capitalism, and his Romantic rebellion against the power of money, are the main sources of his realist clear-sightedness."[8] In short, it is precisely through the romantic and even non-realist aspects of culture that an accurate articulation of the present capitalist totality can find expression. Rather than rely on a strict and oft-too-narrow binary of realism and non-realism as a measure of political valence, Löwy and Sayre put it like this:

Many Romantic and neo-Romantic productions are deliberately non-realistic: fantastic, fairy-like, magical, oneiric, and more recently, surrealist. Yet this does not at all reduce their relevance and importance, both as critiques of capitalism and as dreams of another world, quintessentially opposed to bourgeois society. It would perhaps be useful to introduce a new concept — "critical unrealism" — to designate the creation of an imaginary, ideal, utopian or fantasy universe radically opposed to the gray, prosaic and inhuman reality of industrial capitalist society.[9]

Critical un-realism as a category fits well with the notion of a Gothic Marxism outlined here, and more broadly, with the development of the Gothic novel in English. Despite the horror, despite our *fear*, the world is, at its core, able to change in radical and terrifying ways. There may be those who claim that the Gothic and horror simply represent a kind of fantasy or plane of experience that doesn't necessarily intersect with the real world, but this misses several important points. Perhaps most importantly, imagination and cultural production are historically mediated — the development of the Gothic novel in English is closely bound up with political and social forces, or to put this another way, objects of fear are not removed from our own history. Horror writing developed out of a wider context of political and social factors bound up with real-world concerns around politics and religion.[10] Secondly, imaginative capacity is precisely the catalyst for the transformation of the world through human agency — from religious struggles to revolutionary movements, all have made use of imagination, fantasy, and possibility, whether through the prophetic language of a future paradise or through an innovation of the injustice of the present.[11] This is actually at the core of Bloch's critique of Freud — for Bloch, fantasy, imagination, and even our daydreams have little to do with the past, but are an insight into a kind of utopian impulse of which all of history is the outworking. If this kind of romanticism is anything, perhaps it is best understood as a *Weltanschauung* — a transformative worldview that cuts against the crude, violent realism of capitalist modernity. This is something that Gothic and horror writing has always had the capacity to do.

Generally, the Gothic in the English novel is said to have started 1764, with the publication of *The Castle of Otranto* by Horace Walpole, and functions as the historical forerunner of the more present-tense-minded form we call horror, which has spread across every mode of culture we have. The first edition of Walpole's novel came with a forward by the author, who presents the narrative as the product of his own antiquarianism and collecting — it's a medieval tale that he (Walpole) has simply "found" and presented to the readers. The novel was critically and commercially successful, and Walpole soon brought out a second edition. Here, in the forward to the second edition, he confessed that the novel was fiction — an attempt, as he put it, to bring together the old and the modern forms of romance. In other words, Walpole was trying to synthesise the medieval and early modern chivalric romances of antiquity with the more modern and realist forms of the developing novel. He was, in short, trying to create a kind of critical unrealism. More widely, the early Gothic depends upon the emergent realism of the novel form, while in its content it consistently points to a world beyond the realistic. It is this tension that runs throughout the English Gothic as it develops — the pioneer of the Gothic novel, Ann Radcliffe, exemplifies this in the repeated trope of the *explained supernatural*, in which the noises of ghosts in some distant castle turn out to be the result of servants or some other entirely rational cause. Mary Shelley's *Frankenstein* continues this, with anatomy lessons and modern science colliding with the alchemical studies of Paracelsus, all toward the aim of bringing the dead back to life. (More on *Frankenstein* later in Chapter Three). For the Gothic novel and horror more generally, history is unstable and unfinished — the present constantly shattered by the often-violent return of the past. Despite its formal realism, the Gothic consistently presents and represents dreams and nightmares of a new, horrifying, and different world.

It is this sense of the possibility of a different world that connects the Gothic novel to the other influences of German philosophy and French surrealism. The influence of Schiller, Goethe, and German philosophy in particular on the development of the Gothic novel in English has always been downplayed — this probably begins with Samuel Taylor Coleridge's minimisation of the German *Schauerroman* or "shudder novel" in his *Biographia Literaria* as being essentially derivative of the elegy tradition of English poetry. Schiller's *The Ghost Seer*, with its testimony narrative — aiming to be realistic and convincing — and the plot which is made up of Jesuit conspiracies, spiritualism, and the supernatural, provides so much of the formal and artistic ground of the development of the Gothic as a form. The other influence forming the dark way of being red is Goethe. Goethe's work — in particular *Faust* — was enormously influential for a host of philosophers and authors. In terms of philosophy, Goethe is the largest and clearest influence (other than Marx) on Bloch's own work. From Goethe, Bloch took the idea of *Steigerung* or "intensification," incorporating it into the linguistic style and formal structure of *The Principle of Hope*. As the translators to that work outline:

He develops Goethe's conclusion in "Faust" that "Everything transitory is only a metaphor," and sees the very objects of the phenomenal world as "real ciphers" of the world-riddle, that is, he believes the world contains in metaphorical form the secret signatures of the world mystery that is to be revealed. Bloch had conceived this idea of traces which the world-secret leaves behind it in the physical details of the world much earlier in "Traces," begun in 1917 though completed in 1930, but it is in "The Principle of Hope" that this aspect of his theory is developed into a fully fledged aesthetics, synthesised with the concept of the possible utopian All that, if progressive forces prevail, may finally be attained. Art is thus fundamentally concerned not with the imitation but with the revelation of the world, the process by which the images of the Not-Yet-Conscious are brought into consciousness.[12]

Goethe — and Bloch too — aimed at a human "becoming" whereby the true aspects of the phenomenal world could be glimpsed through the veil. To put the point into slightly more Gothic terminology, the world and all of history are haunted by the possibility of revelation. Not for nothing do even Bloch's critics credit him with the preservation of the tradition of the scorned — the notion that justice is achievable, that the world might be transformed.[13] Here, we can see a connection to another key thinker beloved of the romantic anti-capitalist — Nietzsche. Nietzsche's vitalism and philosophy of action also speak of a world transformed. For Nietzsche, to make oneself anew is a great philosophical and aesthetic project — and the world we inhabit currently is one that is anti-philosophical, leading to a stultifying existence against which one can and *must* rebel. Central to Neitzschean thought is "amor fati" or the love of fate, the notion that one should love the world as it is and not just idly wish for it to be different.[14] This undeniably creates friction with Bloch's notion of seeing the revolutionary possibilities latent in the world as it is. As Habermas points out, the two form opposite poles — "*Carpe diem* can only be realised when the deal of amor fati has been broken off"[15] We can only seize the day, with all of its potential, if we move *beyond* the love of fate espoused by Nietzsche. Yet both were thinkers who moved beyond the strictures of an arid materialism and saw the revolutionary process as not simply a transformation of economic affairs but of the world and a fundamental shift in how human subjectivity comes to experience itself.[16]

This brings up the third tradition we may draw upon for a contemporary Gothic Marxism — the arguments of surrealism and expressionism. The two artistic movements are distinct, although it's reasonable to see them as interrelated, sharing a kind of familial resemblance. Expressionism, in painting most particularly, aimed at the representation of emotion. For the surrealists, reality itself was something that obscured the truth of experience — hence their collective interest in the dream, Freudianism, and systems of magic. Yet these aesthetic interests were in no way in conflict with their politics. As Michael Löwy explains in his essay on the surrealists, the movement was irrevocably committed to a radical, often militant Marxist politics. Löwy explains the politics of Andre Breton as follows:

> Perhaps one might call it a "Gothic Marxism," that is, a historical materialism sensitive to the marvelous, to the dark moment of revolt, to the illumination which pierces, like lightning, the sky of revolutionary action. In other words, a reading of Marxist theory inspired by Rimbaud, Lautréamont,

and the English Gothic novel (Lewis, Maturin) — without losing sight for even an instant of the vital need to combat the bourgeois order. It might seem paradoxical to unite, like communicating vessels, *Capital* with *The Castle of Otranto*, *The Origin of the Family* and *A Season in Hell*, *State and Revolution* and *Melmoth*. But it was at that singular moment that André Breton's Marxism was formed, in all its unsettling originality.[17]

Löwy correctly connects this to the work of Bloch and Benjamin, and to the wider tradition of romantic anti-capitalism. Fascinated by pre-capitalist history, the surrealists (and the idea of Gothic Marxism more generally) seek to go beyond mere nostalgia and use it as a "force in the battle for the revolutionary transformation of the present."[18] Not for nothing did Walter Benjamin find the surrealists an exceptional source of inspiration — it is in his famous essay on the surrealists that he refers to the materialist, profane illumination, and the essay concludes by pointing out that, in the context of the day, it was the surrealists alone who appeared to have understood "the commands" of the Communist Manifesto.[19]

Margaret Cohen takes the term "profane illumination" for the title of her excellent book on Benjamin and surrealism, which establishes the importance and primacy of surrealism and Benjamin's thought for Gothic Marxism. Cohen's definition of Gothic Marxism is well worth pointing to here, as it too provides yet more confirmation of the ways in which the Gothic and horror can offer new perspectives on the relationships between economic base and ideological superstructure:

A Marxist genealogy fascinated with the irrational aspects of social processes... Gothic Marxism has often been obscured in the celebrated battles of mainstream Marxism, privileging a conceptual apparatus constructed in narrowly Enlightenment terms. The Enlightenment, however, was always already haunted by its Gothic ghosts, and the same can be said of Marxism from its inception. An archaeology of Gothic Marxism entails not only reclaiming obscured texts for the Marxist repertoire but attending to the darker side of well-known Marxist topoi, starting with the writings of Marx himself.[20]

Cohen is right to identify Benjamin — and particularly the unfinished masterpiece of the *Arcades Project* — as a key lodestar for developing a theoretical grounding for Gothic Marxism, but drawing from a wider body of thought, across literature and philosophy, allows for a more complete view. The Gothic novel, from the late eighteenth through the nineteenth century, developed its critique of realism even as it incorporated elements of realism into its form. From the tradition of German philosophy, sweeping through Goethe, Nietzsche, Benjamin, and Ernst Bloch, comes the idea of the utopian surplus present in all aspects of culture — traces of the dreams of a better world that Bloch took to be an essential component of all of culture and indeed, of history itself. Finally, from the influence of surrealism and the work of expressionist artists in the early twentieth century came the interest in the past as a source not just of nostalgia but of revolutionary possibility. These three sources of inspiration all contribute to both the critical unrealism mentioned by Sayre and Löwy and the continuation of the tradition of romantic anti-capitalism. However, it's important to return to Bloch's notion of the warm and cool streams of Marxist thought. To make sure that the romantic anti-capitalism of the Gothic and horror doesn't stumble into the fanaticism and subjectivism that Bloch warned against in *The Principle of Hope*, it's necessary to explore the ways in which they can articulate a precise phenomenology of subjective experience under capitalism. Horror and the Gothic need to be able not just to offer a nebulous affect or sense of revulsion but to answer the question of what the violence of capitalism *feels like* to live through. It is this challenge to which the next chapter will turn its attention.

CHAPTER TWO

LIFE AND DEATH IN
CAPITALIST MODERNITY

From Marx himself, to Upton Sinclair, to contemporary writers such as Nancy Fraser and Mark Steven, Marxist writers have always conceived the necessity of a Gothic and horrifying phenomenology in order to explore the question of what it feels like to be a subject under capitalism.

Marx and Engels exhaustively catalogued the various indignities, violence, and degradations that capitalism visited upon the bodies of the working classes. Capitalism is, of course, not a *thing*: as explained at the very beginning of this book, it is a social relation mediated *through* things — objects thus take on a kind of power and, as *Capital* so exhaustively documents, workers are reduced to a kind of thing. This logic seeps into the very structures of our imagination and can be found across cultural production. A good example of the phenomenological experience of this, in all of its anxiety, dread, and panic, is detailed in the great twentieth-century novel *The Jungle* (1906) by Upton Sinclair. From the very first sections of the novel, characters are fundamentally shaped by forces of capital. The guests at the wedding of Jurgis and Ona are there to celebrate the beginning of the American dream, but from the outset, the anxiety of money drives much of the action of the novel, including the very prosaic concern of how to pay off the costs of the wedding. As Jurgis is confronted with the sheer physical violence and horror of the meat-packing industry — violence and horror are, of course, inseparable from the wage labour and exploitation of working people — his understanding of his own subjective struggles gains greater coherence. Narratively, the book closes its loop by having the now destitute and criminalised Jurgis run into a character who was a guest at his wedding. He's invited to a socialist meeting, and it's in finding the wider context of socialism that his own experiences start to make sense. If, historically, the novel was concerned with representing the question of how we should live, Sinclair understands the question more accurately to be how we can *afford* to live. The secret horror of the realist novel of the late nineteenth and early twentieth centuries is the simple, brute fact of industrial capitalism's use and consumption of the very bodies of the working classes.

Times have changed since Sinclair's landmark novel, and arguably the novel form has been superseded by film as the mode via which the collective cultural imagination is both shared and shaped. Horror film, with its unique affective capacity — both integral to cinema as a form and horror as genre — has the capacity to present a phenomenological experience that is attuned to the nature of contemporary class contradictions. If the lines are less clear than they were in the heyday of industrial capitalism, this is not because of any withering-away of capitalist exploitation. If the experience of working in the slaughterhouses of twentieth-century Chicago is no longer that of the majority in the Global North, its violence has not ended; it has simply been moved. One only need think of the poetry of Xu Lizhi, a twenty-four-year-old worker in a Foxconn factory who committed suicide. His poem "I Fell Asleep, Just Standing Like That" could serve as a modern updating of the horror detailed in Sinclair's novel:

> The paper before my eyes fades yellow
> With a steel pen I chisel on it uneven black
> Full of working words
> Workshop, assembly line, machine, work card, overtime, wages…
> They've trained me to become docile
> Don't know how to shout or rebel
> How to complain or denounce
> Only how to silently suffer exhaustion
> When I first set foot in this place
> I hoped only for that gray pay slip on the tenth of each month
> To grant me some belated solace
> For this I had to grind away my corners, grind away my words
> Refuse to skip work, refuse sick leave, refuse leave for private reasons
> Refuse to be late, refuse to leave early
> By the assembly line I stood straight like iron, hands like flight,
> How many days, how many nights
> Did I — just like that — standing fall asleep?[1]

The true horror of the poem is not necessarily just the physical demands of the work in question — just as Sinclair's novel doesn't simply detail the difficulties of working in the slaughterhouses of early 1900s Chicago. Rather, the problem is what this work — naturalised, made to appear as the immutable law of the world — *does* to the one who has to undertake it. The poet has to "grind away" his words, or to put this another way, he has to become the very machine he operates all day. Capitalism still manages to see the body of the working classes as something to be consumed. Even in the era of the service economy, the same problem of the subjective experience of life under capitalism still revolves around the issue of what it does to our bodies. Three of the most significant horror films of the last few years, *The Platform*, *Parasite*, and *Ready or Not*, all show the ways in which contemporary capitalism is not simply a system but an interpersonal force, a traumatic reshaping of subjectivity that one is forced to endure in the wreckage of history. All of the films mentioned above render this process as both metaphor and reality — a move designed to underscore the specifically mediated and constructed nature of contemporary life.

The Platform is a 2019 Spanish-language horror film that started as a theatre project and builds its narrative directly around a single concretised metaphor for contemporary capitalism. The film is set in a "Vertical Self-Management Centre" — a tower block made up of hundreds of cells stacked atop one another. Inmates — or perhaps, residents — are moved from level to level randomly each month, with two to each level. Every day, an opulent feast is lowered on a platform to level 1, at the top, before descending through the rest of the tower. By the time it has descended a few dozen levels, the feast has been reduced to scattered leftovers and smeared remains. Below about level 150, where little food reaches, all you will hear are screams, as cannibalism and horrific interpersonal violence are the norm. Lower still, silence, as those on the very bottom levels simply starve to death. The film follows a young student, Goreng, who mentions to his cell mate that he has entered the Vertical Self-Management Centre for six months voluntarily in order to gain his diploma. In Goreng's case, his cellmate is serving a jail sentence, and the suggestion is that even those who are ostensibly in charge of the running and management of the Vertical Self-Management System have no idea how bad things really are. The obvious and immediate metaphor is one of class striations — and an indictment of trickle-down economics — but it is the details of the film that deepen its critique and show it to be concerned with a precise and contemporary form of neoliberal managerialism.

Firstly, it's worth bringing up Goreng's choice to enter the centre. It is a choice motivated by an object of desire — namely, to give up smoking, read *Don Quixote*, and after six months, gain a degree. To put this slightly differently, he is motivated by an attachment to a possible future state. Attaining education is supposed to get him closer to the life he wants, yet it's this goal and desire for a better life that forces him into the horrors of the self-management centre. His attachment to his diploma is one of "cruel optimism." This phrase, originally coined by the writer Lauren Berlant, refers to a particular kind of attachment or affect — Berlant argued that it was the dominant mode of feeling under neoliberal capitalism. A relation of cruel optimism exists when the pursuit of what we want is actually that which stops us from living a good life. Goreng's pursuit of educational credentials leads him to volunteer, but this is precisely what subjects him to a litany of violence and horror. Indeed, it is only when he lets go of the attachment that initially brings him into the centre that he finds even the hope of something beyond it.

Another important clue here as to what the film is doing is the name of its setting — the Vertical Self-Management Centre. If you are an inhabitant, you are forced to *self*-manage. This is a horrific literalisation of what Mark Fisher termed "responsibilisation" — the idea that systemic and structural problems of contemporary capitalism can't be solved by the state, and so the burden has to be put upon individuals to become better self-managers. Fisher wrote movingly about this in the context of mental health,[2] but in *The Platform* this comes to structure the very means of life itself. If you don't have enough food, it can't be because of any structural reason — after all, so many people have volunteered to be here — rather, it is incumbent upon the individual subject to better marshal their resources. If you need food to survive, you have to take it yourself — there are no handouts here, so if you must, murder and eat the person on the same social level as you; after all, the state isn't going to come along and do it for you. It's this logic that leads Trimagasi, Goreng's first cellmate, to try to strap Goreng down and use his flesh to survive when the pair land on level 171. He is, in short, acting as the perfect neoliberal subject; his constant refrain that his course of action is just "obvious" reflects the further naturalising of the constructed neoliberal condition.

The film makes this argument about responsibility crystal clear in the third month of Goreng's stay. Awaking on level 33, he finds himself sharing the floor with a woman called Imoguiri. She's the woman who interviewed Goreng upon his admission to the centre, and she's decided to participate in it as she's dying from terminal cancer and wants to make a positive contribution before her own death. She claims to have had no knowledge of the conditions in the centre beforehand, and she rations her food and encourages the men on the floor below to do the same. She calls for a kind of spontaneous solidarity — if people can simply decide to be better (if they can self-manage more appropriately), then there will be enough food for everyone. She is, unsurprisingly, rather bluntly rebuffed. Social being — the film understands — is determined by social structures and the Self-Management Centre serves as an extrapolation of Thatcher's famous dictum that there is no such thing as society, there are simply individuals. Imoguiri's expectation of spontaneous solidarity is simply designed to put a smiling face on the old expectation that the starving and exploited lift themselves up by their bootstraps. The complete inability of this approach to even ameliorate the structural problems of the centre is made clear. Later in the film, when Goreng and Imoguiri are relocated to level 202, near the very bottom of the tower, Imoguiri hangs herself, and it is her body that Goreng feeds on in order to survive his time that far down.

You cannot expect a certain kind of subjectivity to just emerge organically; rather, social being is mediated through the social field. Human nature is conditioned and mediated through its social environment. Mark Fisher posited that neoliberalism was essentially a machine for the destruction of class consciousness, and the centre thus functions as a brutal Hobbesian concretisation of that machine. It isn't enough to simply ask, as Imoguiri does, for people to only take what they need. As Goreng comes to realise throughout the film, any kind of basic altruism has to be fought for. In one of his final months, he awakens on level 8, alongside another man, Baharat, who is also desperate to escape. The two decide that, rather than simply ask people to be good, generous subjects, only taking what they need, they will enforce it — with violence if necessary. The two ride the platform of food down, forcing those on the top fifty levels to go without food and handing out rations to those lower down. The result is violence — the final third of the film is often spectacularly bloody, but this spectacle serves to underscore the extent to which subjectivity itself is reformed in this system, wherein for one person to eat, another person has to be starved.

The film ends with the discovery of a child who has miraculously survived at the very final layer of the tower — level 333. Baharat and Goreng have preserved a single, beautiful panna cotta on their journey down, intending to send it back to the kitchen and the managerial figures on level zero as a symbolic rejection of their "gesture of largesse". Instead, they find a child — something apparently impossible in the neoliberal hellscape of the Self-Management Centre. Almost inevitably, neither Baharat or Goreng survive their trip down — but the child is sent back as a herald of the New. Thus, even within this machine for the destruction of class consciousness — a space in which the logic of neoliberalism has infiltrated even into the means of life we need to survive — there remains an ineradicable utopian possibility. Even within the depths of neoliberal subjectification, the world is still haunted by the possibility of the New. In *The Platform*, we can see the extent to which neoliberal discourses of responsibility and individualism reshape subjectivity. Sociality and interdependence can have no place in the Self-Management Centre, and so its inhabitants can only view those with whom they have the most in common as enemies.

If *The Platform* is concerned with the idea of a nascent class consciousness and the conditions which ensure its impossibility, then *Ready or Not* is both a social critique of the subjectivity of the rich and an exploration of the ways in which survival under capitalism can become a game for the wealthy. The film follows Grace, formerly part of the foster-care system, who is marrying Alex, the estranged scion of the successful and wealthy Le Domas family dynasty, who have made their generational wealth through a games business. At the wedding, which is both a celebration and ostensibly a familial rapprochement, a game is suggested. Grace draws a card that reads "Hide and Seek" — she runs off to hide, and the rest of the film is a bloody cat-and-mouse chase as the rest of the Le Domas family try to track Grace down and murder her with a variety of rather antiquated weapons before the sun rises. In due course, it turns out that the family has made a deal with a mysterious figure, Le Bail, who built the family fortune in exchange for the occasional blood sacrifice. Grace manages to escape the family — including her new husband — who all meet a suitably splattery end when they fail to make the requisite blood payment in time.

On the immediate micro level, the film underscores the distinction between Grace and the wider family, reinforcing the point that marriage — especially marriage that cuts across the various class strata of society — is absolutely an economic and political arrangement. Grace's own experience throughout the film is essentially a realisation that love cannot stand against the occultic power of economic position. As the *Communist Manifesto* puts it:

> All fixed, fast frozen relations, with their train of ancient and venerable prejudices and opinions, are swept away, all new-formed ones become antiquated before they can ossify. All that is solid melts into air, all that is holy is profaned, and man is at last compelled to face with sober senses his real condition of life and his relations with his kind.[3]

For the Le Domas family, love is not, at the end of the day, an emotional mode of human connection but just another kind of business. To take this argument further, the film is remarkably refreshing in the way it insists that, actually, for the rich, marriage generally doesn't have much to do with love at all. Alex, through the course of the film, is revealed to be both a coward and entirely economically self-interested. However, shortly after the game starts, there is an important moment. Grace is pulled by Alex into the servants' quarters. Furious, she demands to know why Alex didn't tell her about this family tradition. His reply is that if she had known, she would have left him — the conversation is framed as a moment of pathos, with a sympathetic score, but the reasonable response is that *of course* she would have left. Yet Grace's own position is far from unambiguous — marriage is a product of class structure and not only cements class power and privilege; it's also a means by which a certain class mobility can be achieved. The implied question of much in the film is what would have happened had Grace not drawn the card that mandates a deadliest-game-style hunt to the death. At the very end, though she may have requested a divorce, the family money will now almost certainly pass her way, due to the rest of the Le Domas family explosively exsanguinating.

The film provides plenty of justification for people's subordinating their individual judgment to class position: many members of the Le Domas family are willing to enthusiastically enter into this violence to protect their children or to avoid going back to being poor. Discussion of the film often splits between talking about it as a class film or as a film that deals with the topic of family. However, the actual content of the film is very clear — family is not removed from class structures. The film is a reminder of the degree to which the economic base determines the ideological and social superstructures of human relationships. One need only think of Marx and Engels' infamous point in the second chapter of the *Communist Manifesto*:

Abolition [Aufhebung] of the family! Even the most radical flare up at this infamous proposal of the Communists. On what foundation is the present family, the bourgeois family, based? On capital, on private gain. In its completely developed form, this family exists only among the bourgeoisie. But this state of things finds its complement in the practical absence of the family among the proletarians, and in public prostitution. The bourgeois family will vanish as a matter of course when its complement vanishes, and both will vanish with the vanishing of capital.[4]

One of Grace's muttered lines, "Fucking rich people," underscores the extent to which relationships — *especially* for the very richest — are always already mediated through the economic realm, just as the *Communist Manifesto* argues. Yet the film doesn't simply present this as a rationalistic economic exchange; rather, the subordination of human sociality — of love — to capitalism itself is presented as a game. The aesthetic choice of the antiquated weaponry is designed to be sporting, and the family itself thinks of this part of their business dealings as fun: murder for all ages! Rather tellingly, the film itself is produced by James Vanderbilt (of the American dynasty), whose grandfathers were, respectively, the chairman and CEO of Chemical Bank and the chair of the New York Racing Association. Capital accumulation is hereditary, and if understood as a game, becomes something that it is all too easy to rig in one's favour — at least, up to a point. The problem the Le Domas family run into is their own inability to grasp the occult economy at work in their success, believing that it is natural — just the way the world works. As the film highlights, we are bound up with our in-laws. Much like capitalism, family is not nearly as natural as it appears, made as it is through legal and social structures that exist to facilitate the exchange and preservation of capital. Yet, if we come to understand these institutions of marriage and capitalism as constructs, this opens the door to changing and abolishing them. As the beginning of the *Communist Manifesto* puts it, we're haunted by something, and all the old powers have attempted to exorcise it. Perhaps it's time — as Grace does at the conclusion of *Ready or Not* — to make a deal with the devil.

If *Ready or Not* posits the rich's domination as being the result of an occult bargain expressed in the terms of a (mostly) unwinnable game, then Bong Joon-ho's *Parasite* extends this critique, exploring the ways in which the great game of global capitalism fundamentally reshapes human subjectivity. While *The Platform* details the extent of class structures and internal class antagonism, the world of *Parasite* is less one of predation than it is of necessarily interlocking notions of exploitation and use. All things — people included — have become means to an end. The story follows two families: the Kim family, who make their living in a variety of low-paid, precarious micro-work jobs;[5] and the Park family, who live in a beautiful modernist house and enjoy a lavishly affluent lifestyle thanks to the father's job in an unspecified tech industry role. Prompted by a suggestion from his friend Min-hyuk, the Kim family son, Ki-Woo, talks his way into the Park home as an English tutor for the Parks' daughter, Da-hye. From there, the Kim family inveigle themselves into every aspect of the Park family's life. First, Ki-Woo's sister, Ki-jung, is hired as an art therapist for the Parks' young son, Da-song. Next, the family ensures the Parks' driver is fired and Ki-taek, the patriarch of the Park family, is hired as a replacement. Finally, the Kims manage to dislodge the housekeeper, Moon-gwang, who is replaced by the family matriarch, Chung-sook. The opening half of the film plays out like an Ealing comedy — a kind of upstairs-downstairs farce for the era of contemporary globalised neoliberalism. The Kim family fraud is essentially treated as kind of a joke at first. Ki-jung convinces Da-Song's mother of her bonafides as an art therapist, but all she did was google "art therapy" and make up the rest. The jobs on offer are not particularly taxing and mostly involve the Park family paying for the convenience of *not* having to do things, outsourcing the problem of domestic labour to those they can pay to do it for them. The turning point of the film comes after around an hour. With the Park family away, the Kims get to enjoy the luxuries of the house without having to pretend. There's a telling exchange between Ki-taek and Chung-sook. He toasts to the beneficence of the Park family, pointing out that, even though they are rich, they are still kind. His wife (quite correctly) retorts that he has the connection completely backward — they are nice not despite being rich but because of it. Given their wealth, who wouldn't be? To put this another way, the problem of capitalism is not a lack of manners — the issue with poverty is not its lack of social graces — the problem is the exploitation that good manners can cover and excuse.

Late at night, and in the middle of a rain storm, the exiled housekeeper Moon-gwang returns, begging to be let into the basement to retrieve something she's forgotten. It turns out that in a secret room in the basement of the house lives Geun-sae, Moon-gwang's husband, who has been hiding out from loan sharks. The two have been reduced to a kind of financial spectrality, unable to move out for fear of the loan sharks and the Park family, who have no knowledge of the husband's existence. In fact, in the course of the film, it's revealed that Da-Song had a traumatic encounter with a "ghost," in actuality just Geun-sae, who had gone scouting in the house for food. Moon-gwang and Geun-sae are, in a sense, both parasite and host, a contradiction that can only be solved through their vanishing. The couple are parasitic on the Park family, but they're also the victims of a parasitic financial capitalism that reduces them to the position of being — quite literally — ghosts of their former selves. The world the film presents to the viewer is one of parasitism all the way down to the ground — there is no such thing as a non-exploitative relation, because this is the very essence of how capitalism operates. What is especially revealing about the interaction between Moon-gwang and Chung-sook is Moon-gwang's appeal for a kind of shared solidarity. She refers to Chung-sook as "sister," positing a kinship that Chung-sook violently rejects. The intra-class antagonism intensifies as Moon-gwang comes to realise the relationship between the Kims as a family. In the violent struggle, and as the Parks return, Geun-sae is left restrained in the basement and Moon-gwang is pushed down the stairs and left to die in the cellar. The Kims manage to escape into the night, returning to their basement apartment, which is flooded with sewage and rainwater.

Rather than try to read the film as some libertarian or objectivist comment on the parasitic nature of the working classes in contrast to the benign and wealthy Park family, the film is clear about the Parks' holding an almost ontological hatred for the poor. Park thinks that Mr Kim smells like boiled rags,[6] and they tolerate the Kims only insofar as they do not "cross over the line" and as long as they remember their own servitude and the unbridgeable gap of difference this creates between them; paradoxically, of course, as this servitude is based on a twofold lie — the Kims' own lies to secure their employment, and the wider ideological lie that equates position with inferiority. Thanks to their willingness to lie to the Park family, the Kims actually come to a greater degree of self-consciousness — less as a family than as a *class* — and find their work to be *less* alienating.

Then, of course, comes the ending, in which the film quite expertly extinguishes any hope. Their home flooded, the Kims are told to work at a party for the Park family (a rather brutal object lesson in the differences between how the rich and the poor get to deal with a climate changed by capitalism). At the party, Geun-sae escapes the basement, attacks multiple people, and stabs Ki-jung in front of her father. Mr Park demands Ki-taek hand over the keys to the car while he holds his dying daughter. Later, Ki-Woo — who was also attacked on the day of the party — awakens from a coma to find his sister dead, his mother distraught, and his father missing. Ki-Woo and his mother are forced to live back in the basement apartment in which the family started the film. He realises his father is living in the basement of the Parks' old home, sending out messages in Morse code through one of the lights. The film closes on a downbeat note, with Ki-Woo promising his father that he will earn enough to buy the house one day, freeing his father from his ghostly, parasitic existence. The only way to do this, of course, is to earn lots of money — before anything else, this is what Ki-Woo promises his father will be the great motivation of his life. There is no other way; there is no outside from which to act, and so the film closes the loop with which it opens, reinscribing and deepening the patterns of exploitation. After all, the best way of getting the money is probably to find a job similar to Mr Park's — becoming one of those people who look down on the poor, like his own father, as figures of disgust.

All three of these films showcase how the functioning of capitalism demands a reshaping of subjectivity in subordination to an impersonal set of social relations, staging this imaginative as both physically destructive and terrifying to try to endure. A staid, dry economism (while undeniably useful) cannot sufficiently grasp the psychology and phenomenology that horror, as a structure of feeling, can articulate. A better source for a Gothic Marxism, one alive to the possibilities of horror film, is found in Walter Benjamin's posthumously published fragment "Capitalism as Religion." Advancing on the old Weberian thesis of capitalism being formed by religion, Benjamin argues that capitalism is fundamentally religious in nature. The short piece raises three points, all of which resonate with the three films mentioned. First, Benjamin claims that:

> Capitalism is a purely cultic religion, perhaps the most extreme that ever existed. In capitalism, things have meaning only in their relationship to the cult; capitalism has no specific body of dogma, no theology. It is from this point of view that utilitarianism acquires its religious overtones.

Things have no meaning outside of their status as commodities — we could expand the point to include people — wherein social relations are instrumentalised and mediated between the various networks of commodities. What do you become in the Self-Management Centre? Nothing but a number, a figure that is sublimated to whatever literal crumbs descend from those above. What is marriage in the world of contemporary capitalism? A necessary blood sacrifice that would instrumentalise even love to secure financial continuity. Benjamin makes another couple of claims in the short fragment:[7] that it is a permanent cult, without rest days; that you are always expected to produce, and are never free to rest, never free to be a person, but are always separated from others through what the Parks in *Parasite* refer to as the inviolate line that you cannot cross — one's class position. Finally, Benjamin points out that capitalism does not create absolution; it is a religion without salvation. The only thing capitalism produces is guilt, a continuation and intensification of culpability. And yet, in all three of the films discussed so far, there remain aspects of difference that guilt cannot entirely foreclose.

These films raise moments of possibility — the miracle child of *The Platform* is one. Right at the end of *Ready or Not*, Grace sits on the doorstep, covered in blood, newly rich, and without the burden of her murderous husband. Even in *Parasite*, Ki-Woo's fantasies of having enough money to buy a way out are all representations of a still open and non-teleological future. *Parasite* is easily the bleakest of these films; after all, Ki-Woo's dreamworld seems to presuppose only the intensification of neoliberal exploitation. Yet, as Bloch pointed out in much of his work, daydreams and fantasies are the ground on which we come to realise what we are missing. In all of these films, we are undeniably far from positive endings, but we are haunted by the possibility of something other. This is part of horror's undeniable appeal: the films function as a reminder that the cultural moment is not closed, despite the best efforts of capitalist realism's stranglehold on the imagination.

CHAPTER THREE

THE SOCIAL FUNCTION OF THE MONSTER THROUGH THE AGES

For the first-time reader, Mary Shelley's *Frankenstein* showcases a paradox. The creature is referred to throughout the novel as a demon, a nightmare, and an unforgivable abomination. Victor Frankenstein hates what he has brought into existence. And yet, midway through the novel, Victor and his creature come face-to-face. The creature is articulate, reasoned, philosophical, and reflective, appealing not to be a figure of fear but simply to be heard and acknowledged. How to make sense of this? How to read Frankenstein's monster, who, in the wake of Boris Karloff's performance, so many think of as a mute and shambling figure?

In his influential piece on "monster theory," Jeffrey Cohen posits the monster as a harbinger of category crisis — both a warning and a sign of the breakdown between what were previously thought to be immutable positions and taxonomies. Cohen also argues that fear of the monster is really a kind of desire, and that the monster "stands at the threshold of a becoming."[1] Monsters are, in Cohen's phrase, "our children":

that which we have brought into being. Thus, the category of the monster is a political one — it can be all-too-easily inscribed upon a particular position, or a specific group of people. The discourse of monstrosity is political; in an immediate sense, this can refer to those who are made monstrous, or who are "monstered," by the media, but in a wider sense, the monster as a category can serve as a means by which the imaginative limitations of capitalism are brought to the fore.

There's been a great deal of work on the role of the monster in culture — books like *Monsters of the Market* by David McNally and *Splatter Capital* by Mark Steven are absolutely vital. Yet their work can be built upon — monsters perform a vital and often underappreciated social function, embodying the phenomenological experience of shifting modes of production and the variously traumatic nature of such shifts. Mary Shelley's landmark novel heralds the arrival of the first modern monster; Frankenstein's creature is, after all, a product of romantic-era modernity, from his fondness for Volney, Plutarch, and Milton to his ability to reason and argue before the person who gave him life. While Shelley's own politics and those of the wider romantic milieu were never straightforwardly left wing, there is plenty within the novel and Shelley's wider commitments that offers fuel for understanding the figure of the monster in leftist terms.

Mary Godwin, as she was born, was the daughter of Mary Wollstonecraft, author of *A Vindication of the Rights of Woman*, which attributed gender inequality to the different forms of education received by boys and girls respectively (an issue also addressed in *Frankenstein*). Wollstonecraft had also defended the French Revolution from the criticisms of the conservative thinker Edmund Burke in *Vindications of the Rights of Men*. Mary Shelley's father was William Godwin, a radical political philosopher and novelist, to whom Mary dedicated *Frankenstein* upon publication. Godwin was also the author of his own Gothic novel, *Caleb Williams*, in 1794. Godwin's novel is also concerned with inequality — between the titular Caleb Williams and his employer, Falkland. From the outset, then, Mary Shelley was bound up with the radical politics of the early nineteenth century — with Jacobinism and with the French Revolution. Edmund Burke, her mother's intellectual opponent, saw revolution in France as a "species of political *monster*, which has always ended by devouring those who have produced it."[2] While this quote is the most famous example of the language of monstrosity seeping into the politics of the day, it was a turn of phrase that occurred throughout the revolutionary decades of the early nineteenth century in both pro- and anti-revolutionary politics.

Both Mary and Percy Shelley read extensively about the French Revolution and were deeply engaged with the political philosophy of the day. In the middle section of the novel, Frankenstein's creature obtains his education by overhearing discussion of Volney and Plutarch (two favourite authors of the revolutionaries and radicals of the time). Here, the creature learns of the realities of class society:

I heard of the division of property, of immense wealth and squalid poverty; of rank, descent, and noble blood... the words induced me to turn towards myself. I learned that the possessions most esteemed by your fellow creatures were high and unsullied descent united with riches. A man might be respected with only one of these acquisitions; but without either he was considered, except in very rare instances, as a vagabond and a slave, doomed to waste his powers for the profit of the chosen few.[3]

The novel is remarkably polyvocal, both structurally and linguistically: the nesting-doll-style narrative structure filters the events of the plot through several layers of differentiation. It is the creature's voice that is the most fascinating — they speak back to their creator in the same style of philosophic discourse that Victor sees as exclusively his own. The creature takes seriously the philosophical ideas (and their universality) that Victor Frankenstein can only recoil from. There is a historical echo here of the Haitian Revolution. Toussaint L'Ouverture was directly influenced by the universal ideas of liberty, equality, and brotherhood that developed from the bourgeois revolution in France. As C. L. R. James points out, the first invectives against slavery emerged from the revolutionary liberals like Diderot. L'Ouverture read Abbe Raynal, who nine years before the storming of the Bastille was calling for a slave revolt in the name of the human rights of *all* mankind.[4] The violent revolution in Haiti against the colonial power of France was a fulfilment of the universal values that the French revolutionaries had espoused but from which they had shied away. Frankenstein's creature is the living embodiment — the literal incarnation — of all that Victor espouses through the course of the novel, and yet he can only respond to it with rejection, being unable to accept the true universality of a world in which death itself can be reversed and wherein all living things have the desire for recognition and companionship.

The connection to the revolutionary struggle of Haiti goes beyond the resonances between the monster's own struggle for self-identification and determination, and mirrors L'Ouverture's radicalism, which aimed not just at overcoming French imperialism but at fulfilling the promise of French revolutionary politics. Gothic scholar Marie

Mulvey-Roberts sees the book as somewhat akin to a slave narrative, with the sea-voyage framing device reminiscent of the mid-Atlantic passage, with Frankenstein's creature as the enslaved body. George Canning, leader of the House of Commons and foreign secretary, raised the spectre of Frankenstein just a few years after the novel's publication as propaganda against legislation that would force immediate abolition of slavery.

> In dealing with the negro, Sir, we must remember that we are dealing with a being possessing the form and strength of a man, but the intellect only of a child. To turn him loose in the manhood of his physical strength, in the maturity of his physical passions, but in the infancy of his uninstructed reason, would be to raise up a creature resembling the splendid fiction of a recent romance; the hero of which constructs a human form, with all the corporeal capabilities of man, and with the thews and sinews of a giant; but being unable to impart to the work of his hands a perception of right and wrong, he finds too late that he has only created a more than mortal power of doing mischief, and himself recoils from the monster which he has made. Such would be the effect of a sudden emancipation.[5]

As Mulvey-Roberts notes, Shelley's own politics chimed heavily with Canning's, as she reported to a friend that she was delighted with the compliment that Canning had shown to her by referencing the novel in this fashion.[6] Leaving aside the biographical detail, it is in and through the body of Frankenstein's creature that the politics of the novel are constructed. In an enormously influential essay on the politics of the novel, Lee Sterrenberg argues that the novel is essentially politically conservative, classically liberal, and an implicit critique of the utopianism of Shelley's father, Godwin.[7] For Sterrenberg, Shelley translates the political into the psychological, transmuting political themes and ideas into internal psychological motifs. On one level, the argument does make sense; after all, there is no mass movement, nothing approaching what we might term a properly political politics in the novel, but rather only psychological struggles between and within individuals. The essay also takes rather literally the anti-Jacobin theme of the monster who destroys its creator, and sees this representation as a straightforward Burkean endorsement.

However, the biggest issue is that the essay seems to fundamentally misunderstand the very nature of politics. As the novel understands, and as any leftist politics worthy of the name has grasped, politics is fundamentally lived on the level of the body. The realm of the polis is not the abstract world of Godwinian utopianism, but is fundamentally embodied. Frankenstein's creature is a product of vivisection, literally stitched together from the fragments of the poor and working class that Victor has stolen out of their graves. Even in death, the poor do not get the dignity of peace but are once again pressed back into service. Victor "dabbled among the unhallowed damps of the grave... tortured the living animals to animate the lifeless clay."[8] He aims to create something beautiful but is repulsed by the enfleshed subjectivity he brings to being. The creature, in contrast, comes into existence ontologically bereft, unable to make sense of themselves as a person, Strikingly, the language used shares much with slave narratives, as the creature recounts their life: "No father had watched my infant days, no mother had blessed me with smiles... I had never yet seen a being resembling me, or who claimed any intercourse with me. What was I? The question again recurred to be answered only with groans."[9]

To Victor, his creature is a threat, and in the context of the day, it is the *threat* that Frankenstein's creature represented that was carried into political discourse. Authors have commented at length on the connection to slavery, or on the ways in which the poor and the Irish were associated with the same kind of language used in the novel.[10] However, it's important to ask what the nature of the threat is that the creature poses: that threat is a revolutionary one. Victor, in the course of the novel, destroys the creature's erstwhile bride and companion in a scene rife with the language of the fear of miscegenation, being terrified of a new kind of subjectivity. This is the threat that was emerging — not just in the heroic slave revolts and revolutionary struggles such as the one led by L'Ouverture, but also in a new kind of class society. In his influential commentary on the novel, the Italian literary historian Franco Moretti sees the demands of the creature as essentially reformist in nature, and Victor's responses to the demand for recognition as the most reactionary moment in the novel. This minimises the ways in which the revolutionary struggle at the time was, at least in part, an attempt to universalise the struggle of the bourgeois revolutions to all: less reformism per se, rather, a continuation and extension of the already existing revolutionary project. Yet Moretti also makes the following perceptive point about Victor's creation:

In him, the metaphors of the critics of civil society become real. The monster incarnates the dialectic of estranged labour described by the young Marx: "the more his product is shaped, the more misshapen the worker; the more civilized his object, the more barbarous the worker; the more powerful the work, the more powerless the worker; the more intelligent the work, the duller the worker and the more he becomes a slave of nature... It is true that labour produces... palaces, but hovels for the worker... It produces intelligence, but it produces idiocy and cretinism for the worker. Frankenstein's invention is thus a pregnant metaphor of the process of capitalist production, which forms by deforming, civilizes by barbarising, enriches by impoverishing — a two-sided process in which each affirmation entails a negation.[11]

The decade or so following the publication of *Frankenstein* in 1818 was marked by some of the most seismic changes in European and British history as these affirmative negations intensified. Not for nothing does the great historian Eric Hobsbawm see 1830 as a turning point for historical conditions that culminated in the defeat of the revolutions of 1848 and the subsequent "gigantic leap forward" of capitalism post-1851.[12] Likewise, Joshua Clover sees these decades at the beginning of the nineteenth century as the golden age of the riot-strike, in which the ideology of collective action started to find its emergent potentiality.[13] The poor, the non-white, the exploited, and the enslaved are an amalgamation of bodies forced into exploited labour, and despite the ambiguities of the novel's politics — and the politics of its author — the creature becomes a powerful symbol for the revolutionary potential of the monster. And this is not, as the Burkean conservative would insist, a revolution that would destroy the social order in an orgy of violence and death; that is already the bedrock of the social order, after all. It is the bourgeois revolutionary Victor who meets out violence on the defenceless. Rather, the revolution promised and glimpsed by Frankenstein's creature is a fulfilment and dialectical sublation of the social order: the construction of a world wherein all are included within the universal fraternity of which the Enlightenment liberal spoke, but which they would not extend to all. Just as the revolution in Haiti took seriously, and in some ways fulfilled, the claims of French thinkers that *all* would be included in the values of equality and freedom, so too does *Frankenstein* see that life in all of its embodied monstrousness is something precious. Life, as the creature puts it, may only be an accumulation of anguish, but it is worth defending — especially for those whose form of life is viewed with hostility by the world that brought them into being.

To put this another way, Frankenstein's creature has much in common with the emergence of class struggle and with the rise of the mob in late-eighteenth and early-nineteenth-century politics. The rioting mob is *not yet* the class acting in and for itself, but it is the nascent form of this within a particular historical moment. The mob is, in the Blochian sense, the "Not-Yet" of the working class, a monstrous foreshadowing of what is struggling to come into being.[14] E. P. Thompson, in the magisterial *The Making of The English Working Class*, writes that, at the end of the 1820s, "when there came the climactic contest between Old Corruption and Reform, it is possible to speak in a new way of the working people's consciousness of their interests and of their predicament as a class."[15] Thompson highlights the emergence of a Marxist class-consciousness existing in the British working people; and so the second edition of *Frankenstein*, appearing in 1831, is less a historical coincidence than a reflection of the ways the text itself was both responding to and informed by historical conditions. In the Gothic horror of *Frankenstein*, we can find a new theory of revolutionary power, positioning the body of the downtrodden, the poor, and the enslaved as something that can fundamentally upend the social order. The working class as it emerges in this moment of capitalist development is a monstrous body, a becoming-subject that is a threat to the Hobbesian Leviathan of the state — a threat that will only become more pronounced as the nascent labour movement and emergent working-class identity starts to cohere. It is no coincidence that the novel emerged just as European colonial capitalism started to take its modern necropolitical form. Perhaps now, in a new moment of capitalist crisis, we need to recapture the symbolic and catalytic potential of the monster as that which embodies the hypocrisies and injustices of the current order and points a way toward a better world.

At the end of the novel, Frankenstein's creature is lost in darkness and distance, in the howling void of the Arctic. In a way, the novel as a whole reinscribes a sense of closure (in keeping with Shelley's own liberalism), yet the creature's cultural longevity shows the extent to which the world Frankenstein's creature was forced to endure is still all too present for us now.

In contrast, the nineteenth century closed with the emblematic monster of capitalism's dominance: the vampire. Gothic Marxism has found in the vampire one of its most productive metaphors, one that can connect to thinkers like Marx, to Leninist critiques of accumulation, and to Engels on capitalist predation and social death.[16] If the body of Frankenstein's creature is the racialised and scarred body of the working class, in which "the metaphors of the critics of civil society become real," then Dracula represents the capitalist par excellence. Dracula is, of course, on the surface at least, an aristocrat — a holdover from an older model for arranging social and economic forces. Yet, when the middle-class Jonathan Harker arrives at the castle, there are no servants, no luxuries, and the signs of the brash capital accumulation that marks the private property of the aristocracy seem not to have been impacted by the passage of time. The count does not eat or drink, and he does not even seem to take pleasure in his violence. He is instead pure need. Furthermore, he is interested in property, with "plans and deeds and figures of all sorts."[17] Moretti is very well attuned to the sociological implications of Dracula, and explains it thusly:

> His ultimate aim is not to destroy the lives of others according to whim, to waste them, but to *use* them. Dracula, in other words, is a saver, an ascetic, an upholder of the Protestant ethic. And in fact he has no body — or rather, he has no shadow. His body admittedly exists, but it is "incorporeal" — "sensibly supersensible" — as Marx wrote of the commodity, "impossible as a physical fact," as Mary Shelley defines the monster in the first lines of her preface. In fact it is impossible "physically," to estrange a man from himself, to de-humanize him. But alienated labour, as a social relation, makes it possible.[18]

What is the vampire? What is Dracula? He is, in Moretti's argument, pure capital — resurrected and instrumentalised money — the shape of the capital of 1897, returned from decades of recession and endlessly driving toward monopoly. After all, what does Harker find in the castle? Gold that looks as if it has been undisturbed for years and is now ready to be sent out into the heart of modern capitalism. To be drawn into the orbit of Dracula is to be alienated from one's very self, to be made impoverished as Dracula grows more powerful. Marx himself was well familiar with the vampire metaphor, frequently using it as a way of explaining the relationship between workers and capitalists. This even happens indirectly: some early notes from the third part of the "Economic and Philosophical Manuscripts of 1844" underscore this and could all too easily be describing just what happens to the victims of Dracula's extractivism:

> Everything which the political economist takes from you in life and in humanity, he replaces for you in money and in wealth; and all the things which you cannot do, your money can do. It can eat and, drink, go to the dance hall and the theater; it can travel, it can appropriate art, learning, the treasures of the past, political power — all this it can appropriate for you — it can buy all this: it is true endowment. Yet being all this, it wants to do nothing but create itself, buy itself; for everything else is after all its servant, and when I have the master I have the servant and do not need his servant. All passions and all activity must therefore be submerged in avarice.[19]

The vampire, in this argument, is not motivated by desire but is impelled by the drive toward accumulation and expansion. Dracula is thus, in Steve Shaviro's useful term, a capitalist monster.[20] Yet all this is perhaps a little too straightforward. There is no shortage of writing on the political economy of the vampire, the very embodiment of dead labour that lives only by sucking living labour. However, as Katie Stone points out, while it may be tempting to see the vampire as antithetical to the utopian future beyond capitalism, Dracula does not labour and so Stone sees the vampire as both anti-work and utopian.[21] Stone's argument, which draws from Bloch and more contemporary writers such as Audre Lorde, serves as a counter to Moretti's economism, and is an attempt to separate Marxist theory from the anti-Semitic and racist arguments that accompany the fear of the vampiric miser who comes from outside to threaten the integrity of the British class system. For Ernst Bloch, the drives of human life were never something to just be ignored. To be driven by hunger is to be driven by a recognition of a lack, even if that lack is something only felt and understood physiologically — something in the world is missing and it is this which sends us out into the world. How does Dracula get what he needs? Not through work (unlike the Crew of Light, who toil tirelessly, using all the tools and technology of the time). Rather, the count can simply satisfy his lack in a straightforward and immediate manner, and as a result he is met with disgust for his ability to do so without working. One only need think of the violent, revulsed reaction Jonathan Harker has when finding the satiated count in his coffin:

> He lay like a filthy leech, exhausted with his own repleation... this was the being I was helping to transfer to London, where, perhaps for centuries to come he might, amongst its teeming millions, satiate his lust for blood, and create a new and ever-widening circle of semi-demons to battle on the helpless.[22]

Dracula is, in this moment, at *rest*, and Harker can only respond with visceral disgust. He is, consciously or not, valorising work for work's sake. The second section of Stone's argument is made by linking utopianism to Marxist-feminist ideas about productive labour, care, and the body. Firstly, it must be admitted that the vampire is often instrumentalised to stand in for or represent the figure of capitalism preying on the bodies of the poor, particularly those of children. All too easily, this slides into queerphobic and anti-Semitic attacks on an outside figure in the name of securing the position of white, heteronormative family structures. However, there are two important moments in the novel that are useful for reading the vampire in these utopian and anti-work ways.

The first is the fate of Lucy, and the second is the moment in which Mina is fed by the count. The discussion around Lucy Westenra, one of the first victims of Dracula when he arrives in the UK, often minimises her as an object lesson in the ways that vampirism is a perversion of maternal drives or of female sexual desire. Yet, when Lucy becomes the "bloofer lady" — the figure reported on by the newspapers that takes children away from their homes — there are no weeping mothers in this story. Lucy's relationship with families is quite unlike Dracula's interaction with a mother back in his castle. Rather, the children willingly go to Lucy, imitating her behaviour. As Stone puts it:

> In this reading the children's imitative play is understood as part of a complicated web of utopian longing. The children who are fed upon imagine themselves to be the lady, both beautiful and bloody, who feeds upon them. However, as I have previously noted, the vampiric position they long for — to be able to feed on someone who cares for you despite the fact that you are not a worker yourself — is precisely that of the child. Thus, while the children play the role of bloofer lady, the lady in question is playing the role of a child.[23]

The vampire is thus not a perversion of some essential nature of human subjectivity; rather, the interaction between Lucy and the children is a moment of being made anew, representing a utopian hunger for freedom from the rigidly policed boundaries of the family. Lucy thus gets the freedom to refuse the work of motherhood, and all of this is compounded by the infamous scene in the churchyard when the patriarchs of the novel confine her back to her crypt before violating her body and decapitating her, all in the name of protecting children and innocent women. Similarly, it is well worth extending this reading to the scene between Mina and the Count. The count suddenly appears in Mina's room and both feeds upon her and feeds her. The scene in the novel is rife with a linguistic excess — a moment of high Gothic melodrama:

> With his left hand he held both Mrs Harker's hands… her white nightdress was smeared with blood and a thin stream trickled down the man's bare breast, which was shown by his torn open dress. The attitude of the two had a terrible resemblance to a child forcing a kitten's nose into a saucer of milk to compel it to drink.[24]

What's striking about the passage when read through Stone's framework is the degree to which Dracula is maternal: Mina will become like him thanks to feeding upon his body. The vampire, then, can do something other than simply *take*, and for all the nuance and precision of Moretti's argument, it depends upon the unspoken and tacit assumption that this kind of labour — feeding and caring for those who cannot feed and care for themselves; what Sophie Lewis terms gestational labour — is non-productive. Looking back at Harker's first stay in the castle with the count, Stone makes a compelling point: the count prepares his meals, makes his bed, and cleans up after him, "demonstrating that Dracula's perceived position as an enemy of the worker relies upon an underestimation of the importance of reproductive labor."[25]

Both within and without the familial structure, we find vampirism — after all, Lucy is kept alive by multiple blood donations from multiple partners, and though the novel ends with a new life in the form of Jonathan and Mina's child, the child is given the name of one of the men who died trying to fight Dracula. There is, even here, a communising of care and a sharing and giving of blood.

The vampiric can never be totally extinguished or expelled, but it can be seen as something more than just an external threat and perhaps as something closer to an internal reality. Here, then, we can move beyond the antiquated framework of productive workers threatened by the idle, perverse aristocrat or even of the count as personified capital. Rather, there are utopian traces within the novel, points at which we recognise both our shared contingency and interconnectedness and the idealised freedom of a life eternally liberated from work. There is a much-quoted passage in Chapter Ten of Volume One of Marx's *Capital* which is often brought up in discussions of the vampire; it emerges in the section wherein Marx discusses the working day (a point that's often missed when the quote is decontextualised in discussions of the vampire):

> The capitalist has bought the labour-power at its day-rate. To him its use-value belongs during one working-day. He has thus acquired the right to make the labourer work for him during one day. But, what is a working-day? At all events, less than a natural day. By how much? The capitalist has his own views of this ultima Thule [the outermost limit], the necessary limit of the working-day. As capitalist, he is only capital personified. His soul is the soul of capital. But capital has one single life impulse, the tendency to create value and surplus-value, to make its constant factor, the means of production, absorb the greatest possible amount of surplus-labour. Capital is dead labour, that, vampire-like, only lives

by sucking living labour, and lives the more, the more labour it sucks. The time during which the labourer works, is the time during which the capitalist consumes the labour-power he has purchased of him. *If the labourer consumes his disposable time for himself, he robs the capitalist.*[26]

What does capitalism take from us if not time, extended out into a vampiric eternity? To free ourselves from the capitalist conception of work is to take ownership of our future, to liberate history for ourselves. This is even something that can be seen in modern vampire fiction. At the end of the *Twilight* series, Bella Swan lives an idyllic existence with an interconnected and mutually caring non-traditional family. Immortal and free from the constraints of work, Bella and Edward secure their financial status through investments and by trading stocks. They have no need for productionist conceptions of work; here, the utopian impulse within the vampire collides with the fundamentally neoliberal politics of the *Twilight* series. After all, the freedom from work presupposed here is a utopian idea, but a utopia for whom? The capitalist! Isn't this what every stock market amateur trader and crypto booster wants? To be free from work, to be idle, and to enjoy the spoils of their predation? Again, to return to Marx's 1844 work might be useful. The vampire is a creature of *savings*, and Marx's own language can put this into context:

The less you eat, drink and buy books; the less you go to the theater, the dance hall, the public house; the less you think, love, theorize, sing, paint, fence, etc., the more you save — the greater becomes your treasure which neither moths nor rust will devour — your capital. The less you are, the less you express your own life, the more you have, i.e., the greater is your alienated life, the greater is the store of your estranged being.[27]

Reading our own entanglement with the vampiric allows us to see that the creature is not an outside threat to an apparent inward purity but rather something which we are always already bound up within — an expression of our fundamentally alienated nature under capitalism. We are, as *Dracula* shows, haunted by the utopian possibility of a world beyond labour, a world wherein to be idle is not denigrated but restored to a central right of human subjectivity, and where work is not an expression of alienation but the creative meeting of our own communalised needs. Marx's own son-in-law, Paul Lafargue, sadly little read today, sums up well the nineteenth-century obsession with work that still haunts the contemporary imagination. "Our epoch has been called the century of work. It is in fact the century of pain, misery and corruption."[28]

CHAPTER FOUR

IT'S IN THE BLOOD: BODY HORROR AND FEAR OF THE FLESH IN A POST-COVID WORLD

If the last few years have proven anything, it's that we face a catastrophe of our enfleshed nature. The COVID-19 pandemic, along with various governments' responses to it, has reinforced the sheer instability, vulnerability, and contingency of human life. While some were locked into their homes, working remotely in an intensification of the already endemic levels of social and economic alienation of neoliberalism, others were trapped in low-wage, precarious work and denied any kind of adequate protection from viral infection. Additionally, it is something of a mistake to think of the COVID-19 pandemic as just an isolated bio-medical crisis — rather, as the unfolding events of the pandemic proved, it was bound up with a variety of wider planetary moments of catastrophe, from air pollution to climate change, the rise of microplastics, and a capitalist mode of production that leaves workers mentally and physically exhausted husks.

It was also a moment in which the capitalist state exercised and experimented with various forms of biopolitical control and management, from legislative and legal attempts to limit social gathering to economic interventions around furlough payments to individuals and businesses.

For Xavier Aldana Reyes, one of the leading scholars of body horror, all horror is, in a sense, body horror. But there is also an identifiable and discrete set of aesthetic and affective concerns within horror as a mode of culture around the often-spectacular destruction of the body. This lineage goes from the short stories of Poe to the (abhuman) subjects of H. P. Lovecraft, to the early splatter-punk films of directors like Peter Jackson. Aldana Reyes identifies as "some of its most persistent areas of interest: the body's social inscription, its vulnerability to attack, and its position in an increasingly commodified age that privileges surface and immediacy."[1] Thus, body horror is not simply spectacle — although the visceral thrills are absolutely not incidental — but a way of reckoning with the contradictions and tensions of human bodies. This can include everything from our own much-repressed sense of corporeal fragility to the abject repulsion felt when encountering our own viscera and flesh, or the explicitly political question of what *kinds* of body are made acceptable and which are excluded, marginalised, or seen as monstrous. Frankenstein's creature, discussed in the previous chapter, serves as a good case in point: in the monster, the abjected remains of the poor become a site of miraculous possibility and a threat to the established order. Aldana Reyes uses Katherine Dunn's landmark novel *Geek Love*, which follows the lives of a family of so-called freaks who perform in their own traveling road show, to underscore the ways in which various non-normative bodies are socially determined and inscribed as horrific. In a sense, then, body horror concerns itself with the fragility, mutability, and sociality of human bodies. In our current era of new zoonotic disease, ecological catastrophes, extractive fossil-fuel capitalism, and state biopolitical management, body horror is still urgently relevant.

Drawing from the contemporary horror films *The Sadness*, *Possessor*, *The Beach House*, and *Crimes of the Future*, this chapter assesses the ways in which modern horror still sees the body as both terrifying but also productive and generative in strange and ambiguous ways. These films document how we have become ever more remote from one another as social existence becomes increasingly technologically mediated, leaving the body both more isolated and more vulnerable. Body horror doesn't just explore the contingency and fragility of the body but also its radical and weird potentiality. When our social inscription is brought into question and the seeming integrity of the body as a singular monadic unit fails, what new modes of life can come into being? In all of these films, contemporary horror engages anew the question of what the human body might become when shaped into something new through the very crises which bring our sense of bodily unity and autonomy into question.

The film that deals with these interrelated issues most explicitly is perhaps David Cronenberg's *Crimes of the Future*. In a sense, this high-concept work is the apotheosis of his output over the past forty years and a challenging engagement with the possibilities of radical human transformation in the context of a world blighted by both COVID and environmental collapse. Set in a near future of ecological catastrophe, the film posits a world of radical bodily adaptation and transformation. The human body has become deeply enmeshed in technology and undergone severe physiological alteration. Surgical machines are sufficiently sophisticated as to allow surgery to be performed on people while they're conscious, often as a public social spectacle, helped by the fact that most people seem to feel no pain any more. Even more strangely, a small number of humans seem to now be able to eat and digest plastics, an alteration that attracts both fear and violence from those who cannot do so. The film follows the artist Saul Tenser (Viggo Mortenson) and his artist-partner Caprice, played by Lea Seydoux. Tenser's body suffers from accelerated-evolution syndrome, which causes his body to generate new organs seemingly spontaneously. These tumorous organs are then removed before a surgical audience as part of Tenser's artist practice, a fictional echo of something like *The Reincarnation of Saint ORLAN* by the French performance artist of the same name. The organs are tattooed and registered with a government body that exists to track the appearance and spread of these new human organs. On a personal level, Tenser's syndrome keeps him in near-constant pain, and he uses several biomechanical assistive devices, including a specially designed chair, which twitches and shakes in order to help Tenser digest food.

Over the course of the film, Tenser falls in with a group of radical evolutionists whose main food is a purple candy bar made of processed toxic waste that would be fatal to most people. Tenser ends up taking part in a public autopsy of a child, which is designed to show the child's evolved digestive system, thus demonstrating the government's repression of the truth of human evolution and making Tenser's art both a public act of rebellion and a revelation of the changing body as a symbol of revolutionary possibility. The film ends with Tenser eating the purple waste and, for the first time, experiencing a moment of peace, smiling in his biomechanical chair.

The primary question that the film concerns itself with is one of the driving issues of David Cronenberg's entire career: What *is* the body? And perhaps more terrifyingly, what might it become? What are the crimes of the film's title? The film opens with the death of the child that Tenser will later conduct the autopsy of — the child is murdered by their mother when they are found to have an insatiable appetite for plastics. Yet the larger crime of the future seems instead to be both ecological collapse and humanity's wider loss of control over its physiology. As one of the radical evolutionists says to Tenser, it is time for humanity to start feeding on its toxic waste (seemingly because there is little else for them to feed upon). During a cultural moment when the waste of capitalism is saturated into our very blood, the film pushes this to its conceptual limit. In a world where the body becomes a source of potential transformation, subject to spontaneous change, Tenser's answer is to make the body itself into art. To put this another way, subjectivity requires self-making, and the radical potential of the body is such that it can become something far beyond the bounds of what is taken to be normative.

There is a moment when Tenser goes to a modern art performance where a whole host of artists are exhibiting themselves. There are several old CRT monitors littered around the room, one of which displays the message "BODY IS REALITY." Yet the body is not simply the physical body; rather, as this film and much of the director's other work shows, the body is always already imbricated in wider networks of technology. In *Videodrome* (perhaps the clearest precursor to *Crimes of the Future*), the body is the new flesh, enmeshed in broadcast signals, the flickering light of screens, and the new technology of the VHS (made crystal clear in the famous scene of Brian O'blivion's broadcast). In *Crimes of the Future*, body is still reality, but the body is made and sustained through biomedical interventions. Tenser is kept alive through his organic machines, and the film reveals that human bodies have become so enmeshed with the wastes and plastics of industry as to be indistinguishable from them. In a way, this connects Cronenberg's work with the philosopher of technology Bernard Stiegler. For Stiegler, we are both the makers of and made by technology — technology which then feeds back into our selves in a constant and potentially limitless process of refinement.[2] There is no such thing as a human subject outside of the prosthetic technology through which subjectivity is constituted (in the language of *Crimes of the Future*, body is indeed reality).

If COVID demonstrated anything, it was the essentially unpredictable nature of the body, the lack of human agency, and the ways in which the body is subject to seismic change — all were suddenly disposable. The rise in awareness around issues like long COVID, where the viral infection leaves behind profound changes to the body, from serious problems with breathing and digestion to issues with cognitive function, memory, and brain fog, have brought this home to countless people who may have never previously had to confront their own contingency and bodily fragility. This, combined with air pollution levels in major cities, is proving fatal. The problem is exacerbated in a world in which plastics are found at the very deepest levels of the ocean, throughout the food chain, and even in the very blood of the not-yet born. These kinds of changes require rethinking and re-engagement with issues of human sociality and subjectivity — and while issues of pandemics and pollution are not new *per se*, contemporary cinema is facing the sheer scale of these problems and foreshadowing a nightmare future of complete ecological collapse. *Crimes of the Future* is one of the boldest modern attempts to do so, with even the very nature of desire itself becoming something that is no longer experienced in the same fashion as it was historically. As one of the members of the National Organ Registry (Kristen Stewart) tells Tenser, surgery is the new sex, and Tenser apologetically mutters that he "isn't very good at the old sex any more." What is interesting is that the new subjectivity is not delibidinised, not disinterested in pleasure, and remains driven by desire — there is *new* sex, and a new mode of living to go with it. David Cronenberg's vision of a world that is post-apocalyptic is, in some ways, a remarkably hopeful one — the movie sees new kinds of subjectivity in the possibilities and essential fungibility of the flesh. Indeed, the making of that new kind of subjectivity is the highest (and perhaps only) form of art left for a world of toxic waste.

If David Cronenberg's idea of body horror in a post-viral age is surprisingly hopeful, seeing in the bleak apocalypticism of the present the possibilities of radically new kinds of human becoming, then *The Sadness* both deals far more explicitly with COVID and has a far darker, more fundamentally misanthropic vision of humanity. The film, written and directed by Rob Jabbaz, is set in Taiwan, and follows Kat and Jim, a young couple trying to reunite as the city falls apart due to the Alvin virus, a disease that infects the limbic system, causing those infected to become hyper-violent and act out their very worst impulses. Unsurprisingly, the film is an orgy of spectacular violence, as the infected in the city rampage, torturing their victims with gleeful sadism. The film was written and produced during the Hollywood shutdown, at the high point of the COVID-19 pandemic. From the opening scene, it is far more invested than *Crimes of the Future* in the immediate political response to the virus. Jim talks to a neighbour on his apartment balcony; the neighbour is dismissive of the pandemic. It's all a hoax, a plot by the wealthy elite to fix stock prices, buying low and then selling high. The neighbour says that doctors are all useless, and why worry "when it's only a mild cold anyway."

As Jim gets ready to leave the apartment, he watches a video on his phone: a web-based political show is interviewing a doctor. In vain, the doctor tries to explain that the virus has a potential to mutate and become far more dangerous. The Alex Jones-style talking head interrupts that it's an election year, and wouldn't such a twist be remarkably beneficial to the current ruling party? From there, the rest of the film is akin to a chase sequence as Kat and Jim go their separate ways. Jim stops for coffee, but as the outbreak starts in earnest, he makes it back to his apartment before being attacked by his now-infected neighbour, who gleefully bites off two of Jim's fingers.

Kat is on the subway, and after being hit on by an elderly businessman, she escapes as the infection rips through the passengers in an explosion of violence. The undercurrent of sexual violence is especially uncomfortable and creates an uneasy kind of friction with the libidinal pleasure of *Crimes of the Future*. If David Cronenberg's film says that the body is reality, in *The Sadness* the body is *meat*. The violence of the film, mostly achieved through excellent practical effects work, is a showcase of the ways in which the body can be reduced to so much abject pulp.

For *The Sadness*, the viral infection is about the liberation of sadism. Toward the end of the film, after being stalked by the unnamed business man, Kat ends up beating him to death with a fire extinguisher. His final dying words are a delighted sigh that she is just like him after all. The broad thrust of the film is that latent within all humanity are various kinds of violence that are ordinarily regulated and suppressed through social mores, self-regulation, and — as the film puts it — some mystery of neurochemistry. However, this is a reversal of the actual state of things: the film explains that the infected could no more resist their worst impulses than a person could stop themselves blinking. In the context of the COVID lockdowns, the film stages a dichotomy between isolation, on the one hand, and the worst kind of sadistic sexual violence on the other.

The film is clearly influenced by Garth Ennis's comic series *Crossed* and shares much of its fundamentally misanthropic view of human nature. At the close of the film, Kat and Jim are reunited, and it is revealed that Jim is infected. He talks of his desire to inflict all kinds of violence on her, and says that the infection "feels wonderful." Really there is no new subjectivity here, in contrast to *Crimes of the Future* — rather, what *The Sadness* promises is that we get to be the monsters we always already were. There is a repeated line in the course of the film delivered by a doctor bemoaning the politicising of a pandemic, but the politicising is already too late, given the film's essentially hyper-Hobbesian view of human nature. This is made viscerally clear in the course of the film when the president gives an emergency televised address, flanked by high-ranking military officers. The infection is a threat to the state, and as the president is killed (with a grenade crammed into his mouth by an army official) it becomes clear that, in *The Sadness*, the only real answer is the collapse of the state and the annihilation of the infected by the army.

The final sound of the film is the sound of automatic gunfire, and the final image is the face of a dying and infected Jim. This is really the only way the film could conclude, precisely because it refuses the notion of social being. "You're just like me," says the businessman as he dies, yet this commonality is not biological but determined by the structures of the wider capitalist totality. In a capitalist system, this dichotomy between sadism and victimhood shouldn't be understood as some biological imperative liberated through disease; rather, this violence is capitalist subjecthood at its most basic level. If the capitalist system exists to keep in check sadistic violence, it is entirely reasonable to argue that a new kind of social system would produce radically different human behaviour. In short, if human subjectivity is determined by some innate quality, then misanthropy seems like a sensible conclusion. But if we acknowledge the essentially socially mediated nature of subjectivity, then the issue is not individuals but the systems that make people like the businessman and Kat into the same kind of person.

If *Crimes of the Future* sees body horror as a kind of monstrous becoming, and *The Sadness* sees it as a site of annihilation, another COVID-era horror film serves as a useful counterpoint in underscoring the tragedy and contingency of the body. *The Beach House*, written and directed by Jeffrey A. Brown, follows a couple, Emily and Randall (played by Liana Liberato and Noah Le Gros), who meet an older couple at a beach house. While there, the younger couple try to work through some of their relationship struggles, and the older couple, Mitch and Jane Turner, deal with the fact that Jane is terminally ill and dying. All of the group fall victim to a strange infection caused by microbes released from the water through processes resulting from global warming (making this another film, like *Crimes of the Future*, that connects climate change with infections, illness, and body horror). Once again, this film investigates the nature of the body, but does so in a way that refuses the sadism of something like *The Sadness*.

In fact, the opening two-thirds of *The Beach House* play more like a low-key, indie relationship drama as the two couples interact. What is interesting about this choice is the focus it places on the essentially social nature of the human body. We are never just a subject in isolation; we are made into what we are through our relationships. Filmed and presented in a naturalistic style, the opening section relies on a lot of subtle storytelling and an extensive use of silence to showcase the relationship dynamics between the characters. The younger pair, Emily and Randall, are headed toward a major life change, grappling with their own fundamental incompatibility. Randall is a somewhat typical burnout, whereas Emily is an intellectually curious and ambitious person with an interest in astrobiology. Jane and Mitch, in contrast, are typical, affluent boomers, holding onto some vestiges of cultural capital and their own insecurities, provoked by Jane's terminal illness. This section of the film is, in a word, mundane, comprising a naturalistic unfolding of a familiar status quo presented in myriad relationship dramas and in countless real-life conversations. Yet this all brings to mind a line from Walter Benjamin's *Arcades Project:* "The concept of progress must be grounded in the idea of catastrophe. That things are 'status quo' is the catastrophe."[3] In the midst of a pandemic, in the midst of a strange infection that can spread across the world, normal life still goes on. The great horror is not that there is some microbial infection that can end life, but that, even then, you still have to get up and go to work, or take a weekend away to try to patch things up with a partner.

The horror here is far more low key than in the other films talked about so far. The four decide to have dinner together, during which Emily talks about her interest in astrobiology. She says that life is fragile, and to consider this a body-horror film is to bring attention to the fundamental contingency and fragility of human subjectivity. Sometimes, something so small as to be invisible can just fall out of the sky, or come out of the ocean, and life as we know it comes to an end. Jane, too, is another good example of the film's interest in exploring the fragility of human life: she is dying from a terminal illness, and after the dinner party, the group try edibles for the first time. Jane and Mitch repeatedly say that "we're so grateful to be here with you." Yet, in the morning, Jane's condition worsens: she's now suffering with raw skin lesions and appears catatonic. Emily and Randall find Mitch on the beach, who admits his own inability to cope with what has happened. He then walks into the sea and drowns himself. Here, then, the film uses body horror to underscore the real-world sociological fact that men are far more likely to leave their female partners if those partners are diagnosed with a terminal illness.

In the course of the film, Randall is injured, and in the final few sections of the film, he dies. The audience gets to see brief glimpses of those who become infected. Government officials are either missing or have seemingly abandoned their posts, but the characters all make reasonable and relatively sensible choices. The group shelters together and then tries to find transportation, but when facing an extinction level event that is affecting an entire nation, there's little that individuals can actually do. The film serves as a powerful lesson about the limitations of individualism, echoing the ways in which the COVID pandemic and the response to it depended upon the mass mobilisation of entire populations. The final moments of the film are also worth some attention. Emily awakens in the surf, clearly infected and dying. The final line is "Don't be afraid," spoken directly into the camera, to the audience. The line can be read in two ways: firstly, as a bleak admission of our powerlessness in the face of infection, demanding only our acceptance of our finitude. However, there is a detail here that offers the potential to read the line in a second way, as hopeful: on land, it seems that the infected are transformed into almost Lovecraftian mutations, but those in the sea simply vanish beneath the waves, changed into something new. "Don't be afraid," says Emily at the end, raising the possibility that, by letting go of that Benjaminian status quo and acceding to a kind of radical transformation, we can still find a new sort of existence. *The Beach House* is about the horror of the everyday in the wake of the bodily transformations brought about by sickness, by finitude, and by events like the COVID pandemic.

In contrast, Brandon Cronenberg's film *Possessor* explores the ways in which contemporary capitalism depends upon a kind of psychological exploitation whereby subjectivity is completely subsumed into the continuing operations of the capitalist economy. The film is set in an alternate 2008 in which Tasya Vos (Andrea Riseborough) works as a high-profile assassin. By using a special device and implanting a chip into the mind of a suitable candidate, Vos can take over their consciousness and use them as a murder weapon. Vos separates the host's consciousness from their body by making them commit suicide. Due to the amount of time that she spends imitating others and inhabiting the consciousness of others, Vos struggles with maintaining a coherent sense of self. She has a family and keeps her professional life a secret, but finds thoughts of violence intruding into her day-to-day domestic life. Her handler is the retired assassin Girder (Jennifer Jason Leigh), who sees Vos's connection to her family life as something to be discarded. Despite the emotional toll of each assignment — or "performance," as the film refers to them — Vos agrees to undertake the assassination of John Parse (Sean Bean), who runs a data-mining company called Zoothroo, and of his daughter, taking over the consciousness of the daughter's fiancé, Colin Tate (Christopher Abbott). This mission is only partly successful, with Tate killing his fiancée, but when Vos tries to make Colin shoot himself, he cannot be made to pull the trigger. Instead, Tate stabs himself in the skull, damaging the implant, leaving Vos trapped within his mind and allowing Tate to access Vos's memories of her family. Tate ends up making his way to Vos's home, confronting her husband and child. Both of them end up dead, and the film ends with Vos returning to work, free from the obligations and attachments of familial life.

Considering this film as an example of body horror highlights different facets of how contemporary cinema presents and explores the body. Vos is, in essence, a parasite of consciousness, and her efficacy as an assassin depends upon how easily and effectively she manages to sublimate herself into the role of others. Her role is, in essence, assassination as a service, with her own sense of self being completely plastic in relation to the needs of her employer.

At the end of the film's prologue, during which Vos controls a woman named Holly in order to murder a man, she goes through a selection of personal possessions to establish her own sense of self. From the film's outset, whatever sense of subjectivity Vos has is revealed to be both malleable and fragile. Vos's boss shows her objects designed to provoke memories and restore her sense of self, the most crucial being a red butterfly that she pinned and displayed as a child, confessing that she felt guilty about doing so and still does. Vos asks her boss for some time off to spend with her former partner and child, and has to be reminded that it isn't safe for her to be around them. The very next scene in the film sees Vos rehearsing talking to her child, repeating the phrase "Hi, darling" over and over. At home, she constantly flashes back to acts of violence while having sex with her partner or playing with her son, Ira. The body horror in the film (beyond the use of excellent visceral practical effects) is essentially concerned with the capitalist shift from modes of employment that require subjects to perform certain tasks, to a mode that requires subjects to assume certain kinds of subjectivity. It's no longer about what you do but rather who you are and who you can become. It's no coincidence the film is set in an alternate 2008 — the great financial crash heralded a shift to debt-based consumption, greater flexibility in terms of labour conditions, and the responsibilisation of the individual, coercing them to be both adaptable and resilient, to constantly invest and reshape themselves to be as employable as possible.[4] *Possessor* makes this metaphor concrete: the body horror is not what is done to the flesh; rather it consists in the splitting of the subject's mental life in the name of employment. Even Girder admits that she is too old for the machine and barely recognises herself anymore.

The film uses its strange and surreal imagery to great effect to show the transmission of consciousness between Vos and Colin Tate. The move from one mode of being to another is made literal, and the film shows a melting body that reconstitutes itself as Vos takes over his consciousness. The film further deepens its critique of contemporary labour conditions when Tate/Vos goes to his father-in-law's company office. There, rows of uniformed workers are assigned a desk in a space called "the mine." The workers are expected to wear what looks like a low-tech or early version of an Oculus Rift VR headset. Putting it on, Tate/Vos finds himself in a

VR office with an image of a computer, upon which video clips from around the world play, showing everything from people talking to one another, to others having sex, to children running around with a phone. Tate's job is to catalogue and characterise the type of blinds or curtains in every clip. These clips have been gathered seemingly without the consent of those they feature — one character describes it as a violation.

We live in a networked age in which privacy has become something we willingly cast aside. Smartphones and digital home assistants are almost always listening to all conversations, and social media posts are scraped for algorithmically driven, targeted advertising. The brief sequence showing Tate in the mine provides an insight into the current condition of AI and automation, whereby large language models or data sets appear to be generating insights but are only generating conclusions based on human input and micro-work. Increasingly, a lot of this real-world labour is outsourced to poorly paid and exploited workers overseas, whose own labour is made invisible in order to maintain the illusion of automation. The model of work that the film explores has real-world echoes, from the panopticons of Amazon fulfilment centres to the data-trainers of the Philippines.[5]

However, the Vos-Tate connection is deeply unstable, with Tate troubled by extreme hallucinations as the film makes visible a kind of splitting of the subjective — or, to put things in more Deleuzo-Guattarian terms, a kind of schizophrenia. After all, Vos is quite literally the embodiment of capitalist reterritorialisation: the aim of her "performance" is not just the death of John and his daughter Ava, but the gaining of access to the company he runs and the data that comes with it, all for the benefit of her own employers. Vos gets inside Tate's head, but ultimately the aim is to be able to get inside everyone's. As one of Tate's friends rather bluntly puts it: "I jerk off every day in front of my webcam so Zoothroo knows exactly what brand of vibrator I'm using." The body horror of contemporary media culture is that we are always inviting others inside our heads, to commodify our consciousness and sell off our desires, dreams, and thoughts to targeted advertisers. Another good example of this is the moment of "recalibration" that Girder asks Vos to undertake just before the dinner party at which Tate is supposed to kill his fiancée and her father. Through a device and an implant in Tate's skull, the viewer sees Tate/Vos go through the entire gamut of emotions, from a rictus grin, to fear, to tears. The dream of the neoliberal society of control is precisely this: to use technology as a means for neurological manipulation.

After the attack on John and Ava (which includes a wince-inducing scene with a fireplace poker), the back third of the film is essentially an externalisation of the internal struggle within the Tate/Vos subject. Tate jams a shard of glass into his skull, damaging the implant placed there and preventing Vos from severing the connection that links them on the level of consciousness. The editing in this section becomes increasingly important to the film's meaning, juxtaposing and layering images of violence committed by "Tate" with flashes of Vos's own domesticity. "I should have stayed with Michael," says a terrified and confused Tate — when another character asks, "Who's Michael?" the only response that Tate can give is a confused "I don't know."

Whereas earlier body-horror films saw the body and its interactions with technology as a site of mechanical possibility, the body here is a psyche. As in *Crimes of the Future*, body is still reality, but the consciousness of the body is the means by which that reality is mediated and thus controlled.

A lifeline from Vos's organisation arrives, and in a sort of fugue state, Tate hallucinates himself placing a mask of Vos's face over his own: once again, the film literalises the mechanisms of psychological control. The ending of the film is perhaps its most bleak point. After tracking down Vos's family once their consciousnesses have bled into one another, Tate is killed along with Michael and Vos's son. She returns to work, and once again Girder takes her through her possessions. Upon coming across the butterfly, Vos makes no comment. In a way, Vos has become the perfect neoliberal employee — endlessly flexible and malleable, able to perform any kind of subjectivity required, and freed of both memory and guilt. With her family dead, Vos's fate is the same as Girder's: neither is able to look herself in the mirror, and they are no longer able to recognise themselves at all. COVID has only accelerated the subjective plasticity that the film details; as work has become more precarious (or in the euphemism of capital, "flexible"), there is an increasing drive to make oneself an ever more adaptable subject. Unlike *Crimes of the Future*, *Possessor* doesn't see the body's potential for a kind of becoming; rather, it dwells on the acceleration of neoliberal discourses of psychological control. This is a slight shift in body horror, away from the physical immediacy of the subject and toward the ways in which subjectivity is a matter of enmeshment with wider political forces. This shift connects *Possessor* to films that directly confront the neoliberal condition (*Parasite* being an excellent example discussed in Chapter Two). In *The Sadness*, humanity is so much meat, disguising a maelstrom of sexual violence, whereas in *The Beach House*, it is in our very mundane existence that we come across the true horror of the body: namely, our own finitude, fragility, and human contingency. What is needed is a means of making sense of the human subject that doesn't simply reduce it to dumb matter, but like these films, understands the human subject as both process and potential.

CHAPTER FIVE

WITCHES, AND BEING A MONSTER TO CAPITALISM

In 2018, there was a strange story in the American press. In the wake of Brett Kavanaugh being appointed to the US Supreme Court, a small self-described metaphysical boutique and bookshop from New York announced they would hex the new Republican justice with the aim of hurting him. In response, Father Gary Thomas, the exorcist for the diocese of San Jose, California, told a Catholic newspaper he would host a special mass of protection for the new Justice. The co-owner of the bookshop told *Newsweek* that they were "basically antifa witches."[1]

Just a few weeks earlier, the newest book by Sylvia Federici, *Witches, Witch-Hunting, and Women*, was published — in their review, writer Jude Doyle said that the work was monumental, ever more relevant, and would "take your head apart and put it back together."[2] The previous month, the remake of *Suspiria*, Dario Argento's landmark film about a coven of witches, was released.

In the runup to the 2016 US presidential election, images of Hilary Clinton as a witch were everywhere on social media, and in an infamous viral rant, the conspiracist radio host Alex Jones said that Clinton was a demon-possessed monster who both reeked of sulphur and wanted to destroy the world. In the context of the Trump presidency, Trump's own well-publicised misogyny, and the wider rightward cultural shift of which Trump was himself a symptom, the witch became a renewed feminist symbol of a resistance to patriarchy. Additionally, women were made into witches, made monstrous by the same patriarchal structures that sought to violently impose limitations on women's behaviour. Even Taylor Swift would sing about the witch trials on her 2017 album, *Reputation*, explaining that:

> They're burning all the witches, even if you aren't one.
> They got their pitchforks and proof,
> Their receipts and reasons.
> They're burning all the witches, even if you aren't one.
> So light me up…[3]

For the novelist and former classicist Madeline Miller, the label of "witch" is never simply about misogyny, but about power; it is a political tool and device of patriarchal authority for making sure that women are kept in their place.[4] To label a woman a witch is not just a punishment but a recognition of them as a threat to the order of patriarchy. Again, in a cultural moment of right-wing politics and misogyny, taking on the label of being a witch is a political gesture, and this is an aspect of the witch revival post-2016. The novelist Trish Thawer's novel *The Witches of Eastbrook* appeared in late 2015, and a line from the novel, "We are the daughters of the witches you couldn't burn," went viral as a statement of feminist solidarity, appearing on everything from protest signs at women's marches to baby onesies you can buy on Etsy.[5]

Here, the political valence of the witch as a label was riven with an undeniable tension: the witch is not only a powerful symbol or identity but a great branding exercise, primed for co-option back into the structures of capitalism.

The aim of this chapter is to argue for the radical potential of the witch as it returned in popular culture over this last decade, to free it from the capitalist kitsch that has co-opted the witch in order to sell it back to women, and to argue that the witch can serve as a model for a life outside of the disciplinary oppression of capitalism. What this calls for is not a feminism that can be commodified, but a feminism that understands that the witch both represents a *threat* to the social order and instantiates a brand-new world. Therefore, drawing from *The VVitch* (2015), *Suspiria* (2018), and Paul Preciado's *Can the Monster Speak*, a Gothic Marxist approach allows for the construction of not just the monstrous feminine (to borrow a phrase from the theorist and film scholar Barbara Creed), but of a monstrous feminism. This would be a feminism that is trans-inclusive, one which abolishes the family form, and which stands outside the normative structures of heteropatriarchal capitalism to bring something radically new into being.

In a sense, of the texts under discussion, *The VVitch* makes this argument about the nature of the witch most clearly, and grounds its own horror precisely in the ways that the witch is a threat to the religious and patriarchal forces that shaped the early American colonialist project. The film is deliberately naturalistic, using sets constructed to be period accurate and a script redolent with Biblical language. Even the subtitle of the film, "A New England Folktale," purposefully positions the film as real: the witch is not just a fictional construct but a formative historical reality. The film follows a devoted, almost fanatically religious family of Puritan settlers who are banished from a settlement plantation and choose to go into the woods to set up a farmstead. The family is made up of the patriarch, William (Ralph Ineson), his wife Katherine (Kate Dickie), and their five children: Thomasin (Anya Taylor-Joy), Caleb (Harvey Scrimshaw), Mercy (Ellie Grainger), Jonas (Lucas Dawson), and baby Sam (Axtun Henry Dube and Athan Conrad Dube). When they arrive, the woods immediately reveal themselves to be a dark and hostile place, and the baby goes missing, taken by the witch in the woods.

Both Thomasin and Mercy somewhat jokingly claim to be the witch: Mercy sings strange chants to the family goat, the demonically possessed Black Phillip, and Thomasin eventually signs her name in the Devil's book, joining a coven of witches who dance together under the starry night sky. There is a witch half-glimpsed at various points throughout the film, but as Elizabeth Parker points out, the witch exists here as a certain mode of relationship between nature and geography. The witch here is less a direct opponent than an embodiment of the various vulnerabilities of the patriarchal, colonialist, and religious project that the family exemplifies.[6] After all, what is nature but something that the family has to go and subdue — the film's insistence on historical verisimilitude places it within a longer Gothic tradition of seeing the woods as fundamentally anti-Christian. The obvious literary antecedent here is something like "Young Goodman Brown," the famous Nathaniel Hawthorne story, in which a walk through the woods reveals the natural world to be anti-Christian, home of a midnight Sabbath where the titular character comes face-to-face with Satan.[7]

To go out into nature is to have to work to survive — *The VVitch* is full of scenes of domestic and reproductive work, whether children working on the farmstead, hunting in the woods, or the scenes of William compulsively chopping wood. As Sylvia Federici points out in her landmark *Caliban and The Witch*, the witch represents an occult economics whereby what is needed can be obtained without work (here the witch connects clearly to the reading of the vampire proposed in Chapter Three).[8] The work in the woods is hard, dangerous, and profoundly unfulfilling, and as the film progresses, nature itself is presented as fundamentally hostile to these attempts at domination and exploitation, with the family's crop literally rotting before their eyes. The demon-possessed Black Phillip sees clearly that the life Thomasin is promised is one of unrewarded (re)productive labour, religious and theological submission, and continued involvement with a dominating and extractive capitalism that sees the natural world as something to be forced into an ultimately destructive ecology. Thus, the family, the world of colonial violence, and the patriarchy of Christian colonialism are all institutions and modes of life that one can refuse, and it is this act of refusal that so terrifies the forces that would keep Thomasin within the farmstead. "Woulds't thou like to live deliciously?" is what Black Philip asks, and at the end Thomasin literally ascends, a part of a new communal mode of living.

The horror of *The VVitch* is in its atmosphere, wherein the world is presented as possessing a terrifying, non-material reality behind it. I've written elsewhere about the persistence of this theological materialism within the ideology of a Calvinistic Christianity,[9] whereby the relationship between the world and the subject always conceals a more profound spiritual reality. What *The VVitch*, and Thomasin's eventual choice, reveals is that the world cannot be made to conform to the oppressive structures of people like William. To choose witchcraft is to be enmeshed within nature, a web of life that opens into new ways of being, exemplifying the degree to which the structures of capitalism can never completely subordinate the outside, and thus never completely foreclose the possibility of a new world and utopia.

The possibility of utopia — or, to put it another way, the attempt to resist the capitalist foreclosure of utopia — inevitably collides with the question of politics. In *The VVitch*, Thomasin's choice of a delicious life is necessarily individual (even if she enters into a new communal structure), and given the wider family move away from the settlement, plus the film's broader alignment with nature, she is a witch who is, in a sense, pre-political. In contrast, Luca Guadagnino's 2018 *Suspiria* — described as an homage to Dario Argento's classic giallo — is a film explicitly concerned with the witch as a mediating force between the realms of politics and aesthetics. Argento's film was an explosion of colour, while the 2018 film is bleak, shot with a wintery palate and subdued tones, its soundtrack provided not by the prog-rock band Goblin but by the far more pessimistic and melancholic Thom Yorke.

While Argento's film mostly avoided the explicit politics of its setting, preferring instead a focus on psychodrama, the creative team behind the new version aimed to make their film far more politically engaged. Within the film, the coven both politicise their aesthetics and enact a response to the fundamentally Gothic nature of the politics of the day. The film, set as it is at the tail end of the German Autumn, is directly in conversation with the revolutionary struggles of the 1968 generation and the questions of violence and confrontation with the state that preoccupied revolutionary movements like the Rote Armee Fraktion, otherwise known as the Baader-Meinhof Gang. As Alexander Howard and Julian Murphet put it in their excellent article on the film, the "presiding West German spirit of 1977 was the journalist-cum-Rote Armee Fraktion (RAF) militant Ulrike Meinhof."[10] Meinhof was a journalist and intellectual whose own political commitments drew her toward the revolutionary politics of the radical left; her own writing speaks of the fundamentally Gothic and haunted nature of the late-1970s extremely well. The passage below is from a piece written in 1961, entitled "The Hitler within Us":

> The narrowing gap between the fronts of history and politics, between the accusers, the accused, and the victims haunts the younger generation. This generation was not involved in the crimes of the Third Reich or in determining the direction that was taken in the postwar period; it has grown up with and into the arguments of the present, entangled in the blame for something it is not responsible for. The realization that this generation is innocent cannot, however, be used as an instrument by those who want to refuse young people the right to have their say about history; nor does it free this generation from facing the responsibilities of the present.[11]

The politics of West Germany were haunted — haunted by the victims of the Nazi regime but also by the incompetence, reluctance, and inability of the political and intellectual structures of the day to confront both German complicity and the degree to which Nazis were still in positions of power throughout German society. The official policy of the time of "working through history" sought to close the book on the past using commemoration and memorialisation, but as Meinhof pointed out, fascism is a ghost that has to be exorcised, or to put the question in terms that Deleuze and Guattari would employ in their landmark work, *Anti-Oedipus*: how do we get rid of the fascist inside our own head? At the opening of the film (which begins with cries of "Long live Meinhof," despite Meinhof already being dead), the young dancer Patricia bursts into the office of the analyst Dr Klemperer (played in heavy makeup by Tilda Swinton, who also plays Madame Blanc, a senior figure in the dance troupe), raving about witches. Later, in conversation with another member of the troupe, the sensitive Sara, played by Mia Goth, Dr Klemperer argues that "you can give someone your delusion… That's religion. That is the Reich."

Just as with the coven, the Reich too had its metaphoric titles, its esoteric rituals and symbolism. In a sense, then, the coven is a synecdoche for the political and social totality of West Germany. The dynamics of the coven serve as a polysemous allegory for the various contradictions of the moment and the wider tension between aesthetic expression and politics more generally. The doomed dancer Patricia is deeply committed to militant causes, and apparently leaves the coven to go — as Madame Blanc puts it — to "fill bottles with petrol underground." Klemperer compares the coven to a revolutionary organisation going through a power struggle (in an echo of the real-world conflict between the various factions of the RAF as well as of the broader antagonism between revanchist capitalism and the revolutionary avant-garde). At the same time, in the relationship between the coven and Dr Klemperer, there is a wider point about the relationship of the individual to history. The doctor is guilt-ridden at his own failures to save his wife during the war, and spends much of his time in the film passively observing, the very model of therapeutic impartiality. At the climax of the film, he becomes a spectator to the spectacularly bloody ritual of the coven — all the while protesting his own innocence.

In the character of Klemperer, the film reckons with the culpability of passivity. Fascism was never confronted by Klemperer — it couldn't be — and he paid his own terrible price; after all, as Chapter Six will argue, all hauntings are inescapably bound up with grief. As the matrons of the coven bitterly remind him, he had plenty of time to get his beloved Anke out of Berlin, but failed to do so. As a result, Klemperer is doubly haunted: by both the ghosts of his own lost love, and the fascist ghost which is still, quite literally, *embodied* in the art and institutions of the present.

As pointed out in the discussion of Frankenstein's creature, the monster's body is the site of politics, and here, the film adds complexity by having both fascism and magic be expressed physically. Much of this finds articulation in the coven's performance of the film's central dance piece — *Volk*. The term is profoundly loaded, with its links to fascist notions of the superior people, and serves as a good example of what a fascist politics does to the body. After winning the role of the lead through her impressive audition and literal destruction of the distraught Olga, Suzy Bannion (a young American) is seduced — at least so it seems — by the feminist enclave the company represents. On stage for *Volk*, clad in red ropes, the troupe work through the ritual choreography. Joining late is Mia Goth's Sara who has had her legs broken by the matrons of the coven as a punishment. Stumbling onto stage, she robotically goes through the motions of the choreography in increasing pain, until she collapses, screaming in agony and breaking the spell over the audience. Internal to the text of the film, both magic and fascism are, at their core, tools for the disciplining of the body. In this, the film makes a trenchant critique of the ways in which fascism instrumentalised the body for its own ends, even in such an apparently apolitical and non-ideological form of art as dance. Howard and Murphet connect this disciplinary function to the ideologically complex role of dance in Germany throughout the twentieth century, drawing attention to how it would be a mistake to

> imagine that modern dance, like other art forms of the period—theatre, literature, painting—enjoyed some putatively "pure" dissociation from National Socialism during the 1930s—that it was labeled "degenerate" or hounded into exile, for instance... The history of modern dance in Germany is a deeply compromised one, and that compromise is felt in the radically unstable corporate image of *Suspiria*'s dance academy: a militant feminist collective that hungrily eats the bodies of the young to perpetuate its own internal power structure, and in so doing masks its complicities with fascism as the benignity of a utopian enclave.[12]

The final point they make is an important element for a Gothic Marxist critique of fascism: Bloch, in his magisterial *Heritage of Our Time*, recognised that fascism was not some mistake of ideology but offered a utopian vision of possibility to the disaffected strata of society, constructing his book as a sociology of Weimar Germany to explore how the fascists could appeal to the various sections of the population. In his later book, *The Principle of Hope*, Bloch explicitly commented on the kinds of expressionist dance practiced by the troupe — even mentioning one of the choreographers that Swinton modelled her character on. For Bloch, expressionist dance was inescapably ambivalent, "partly carried not to distant seas, but into the local bloodlake of fascism."[13] For Bloch, the expressionist movement was, at least in part, Dionysian, constituting a leap beyond the gravity of the present, but one that could never overcome its own imperialist history. In light of Bloch's comment, Blanc's lines to Susie take on new significance:

I don't know how aware you are of what times we lived through here forty years ago... We learned at great cost through those years the value of the balance of things. Every arrow that flies feels the pull of the earth, but we must aim upwards. We need to get you in the air...

Bloch's analysis is borne out entirely in the conclusion of the film: the whole coven ends up precisely in the bloodlake of fascism, at first triumphant that the ritual will succeed and that Markos will get to inhabit the body and consciousness of the young American dancer. Then comes the reveal, there in the heart of aesthetic fascism, that Suzy is none other than the embodiment of Mother Suspiriorum — a witch of godlike powers who precedes any historical notion of God or the Devil. The witches of the coven who sided with Markos are all killed in a spectacular orgy of violence, a grand guignol explosion of blood that the survivors will have to clean up. In contrast, Mother Suspiriorum treats Olga, Patricia, and Sara with gentleness, granting them their wish for a speedy and painless death. In the context of the film's anti-fascist concerns, the revelation of Suzy's identity allows her to function as a Messianic figure — the vanquisher of the Antichrist that Benjamin wrote of in "On the Concept of History." The praxis of the RAF fails — the film closely follows the Lufthansa hostage situation — but in contrast, Suzy/Suspiriorum manages not only to undo the damage of present fascism by delivering Olga, Patricia and Sara to the release of a much-wished-for death, she is also able to stage a genuine confrontation with the guilt and ghosts of history.

At the very end of the film, Suzy goes to see Klemperer and gently explains what happened to his long-lost love. Using her magical abilities, she takes away his memories, saying, "We need guilt. And shame. But not yours." Klemperer has a seizure, and comes around confused, but with the painful memories of the past forgotten. If his own guilt and shame isn't needed, the film argues that it is the survivors of the coven that should feel that; they are last shown covered in blood and guts, scrubbing the floors. The witch in this film is not simply an object of female empowerment (though the film's inclusion in the "'Good for Her' Cinematic Universe" certainly suggests this is a powerful aspect of what makes the film engaging to its audience).[14] Rather, Suzy (and her power) functions as an anti-fascist intervention into history. This is not to say the film operates as straightforward leftist propaganda, but it shares much with the concerns and sympathies of the RAF. The witch, through horror, becomes a monster, a partisan of history that both intervenes in the present and at the same time allows for an engagement with the past that recognises the ways in which we are still haunted and guilt-ridden by that which is no longer present.

Luca Guadagnino makes dance the language of witchcraft: the monster speaks as a speech-act into both the subjectivity of the lived moment and history. The commune of witches is akin to the militant cell or revolutionary cadre, bodies acting in the world across both social and political fields, just as much as they do on the performance stage. So we can consider the witch as not just refusing or negating the possibilities of a norm that produces violence and misery — as in Thomasin's case in *The VVitch* — but as making a positive choice that both redeems the suffering of history and creates a new potential future. *Suspiria*, with its emphasis on mothers, and on the transferences of desire and politics, is often read psychoanalytically. Can the monster speak? And if so, what might happen if, within psychoanalysis, a new monster is found?

It is this question which motivates Paul Preciado's speech-essay-polemic *Can the Monster Speak?*, originally delivered to the Académie de psychanalyse de France and the École de la cause freudienne. Preciado was drowned out as the audience laughed or heckled — one member of the crowd even shouted, "We shouldn't allow him to speak, he's Hitler." Preciado, a trans, non-binary man, was unable to complete his planned speech. The speech was written and published the next year. The book serves as a powerful critique of the psychoanalytic establishment, and as a model of the ways in which monstrosity as a discourse does not simply extend to modes of cultural analysis, as with *Suspiria* or *The VVitch*, but to politics more generally. With *Can the Monster Speak?* and its call for a solidarity of the monstrous, what emerges is a Gothic politics, escaping from the discursive imprisonment of normality and headed toward a monstrous becoming.

From the epigraph, the book immediately sets the tone, so it's worth reproducing in full:

What am I doing here? I have come to terrorize you! I am a monster, you say? No! I am the people! I am an exception? No! I am the rule; you are the exception! You are the chimera; I am the reality!'

— Victor Hugo, *The Man who Laughs* (1869),
quoted by artist Lorenza Böttner in her
thesis "Handicapped?" (1982)

The general argument of Preciado's speech is that trans identity is something which the language of psychoanalysis is unfit to address and that, furthermore, psychoanalysis is discursively bound up with the logic of sexual and gender binaries and hence incapable of responding to a growing global shift in the epistemology and practice of how sex and gender difference are embodied and lived out. This broader problem stems from the false universalism of psychoanalysis's deeply Eurocentric (ergo colonialist, racist, and hetero-patriarchal) paradigms of thought. The literary antecedent quoted from towards the beginning of the text is from an under-appreciated Gothic author, Kafka, and the short story "A Report to an Academy." The text is "an account of the life I [the text's narrator] formerly led as an ape."[15] The ape, named Red Peter, has come to self-consciousness, speaks in the educated manner of the academy, and yet remains what they are. Just like Red Peter, Preciado speaks in the language of the academy, here the language of psychoanalysis, turning the discursive techniques of Freud and Lacan back upon themselves and their descendants.

In an echo of *The Witch*, Preciado begins with the act of refusal:

My predecessor, Red Peter, claimed that he "beat his way through the bushes," and that is precisely what I did, I beat my way through the bushes of academia... And it was doubtless thanks to my status as a "doctor" that I saw the journey become simpler, although for most trans persons it is a journey that represents a formidable ordeal: the task of getting new identity papers in a binary society. After a number of visits to various psychologists who could award me the "good transsexual" certificate that would allow me to get new identity papers, I quickly understood that there were two paths open to me: the pharmacological and psychiatric route to domesticated transexuality and, with it, the anonymity of normal masculinity or, on the other hand, and in opposition to this, the spectacle of political writing. I did not hesitate. Normal, naturalized masculinity was nothing other than a new cage. Those who enter will never leave. And I chose. I said to myself: speak publicly. Don't silence yourself. And so, of my body, my mind and my monstrosity, of my desire and my transition, I made a public spectacle: yet again, I had found a way out...[16]

What does it mean to find a way out? Firstly, Preciado refuses the notion of referring to oneself as a body — he uses the term "somatheque," "a living political archive." To transition means to become a monster in Preciado's terms, and this carries with it an immense political charge. Preciado's points are communicated with almost manifesto-like clarity and polemical force:

The monster is one who lives in transition. One whose face, body and behaviors cannot yet be considered true in a predetermined regime of knowledge and power... To transition is to establish a transversal communication with the hormone which erases or, better still, eclipses what you call the female phenotype and allows for the awakening of another genealogy. This awakening is revolution. It is a molecular uprising. An assault on the power of the heteropatriarchal ego, of identity and of name. The process is a decolonization of the body. It is the potential revolution inherent in any process of transition that terrifies normative psychology and psychoanalysis.[17]

The idea of awakening as revolution shares some common ground here with Frankenstein's creature coming to self-consciousness, but Preciado's vision sweeps across the whole violent logic that seeks to endlessly assert that one can be either *this* or *that*. This logic of strict taxonomies — the network of heteronormative labels from which Preciado made his own escape — is underpinned and enforced through hegemonic disciplinary social force. This same determining logic connects extractive ecological destruction, colonialism, and the imperialist stage of capitalism. What is particularly noteworthy about Preciado's speech-slash-polemic philosophical monstrosity is that he does not attempt to inscribe a more true or universal universality. Rather, the aim is to deconstruct the hegemony of psychoanalysis, ensuring that what he terms the "sexual subaltern" is not subsumed into the discourse of sexual difference. It is for precisely this reason that he describes himself as a sophisticated monster, capable of using the language of psychoanalysis to escape its discursive limitations.

What does this mean for a Gothic politics? For Preciado, this monstrous solidarity is the ground of genuine freedom: "To live beyond the patriarchal-colonial law, to live beyond the law of sexual difference, to live beyond sexual and gender violence is the right that every living body, even a psychoanalyst, should have."[18] Preciado's call for a radical freedom — for the right to *become* — also shares some common ground with the wider project of Gothic Marxism. As the philosopher Adam C. Jones puts it in their series of aphorisms on Gothic Marxism: "Gothic Marxism affirms the monstrous universality which is monstrous and universal not because it is hegemonic (neither in actuality nor in rationality), but because it is insurgent — absolute particularity."[19] In a sense, we might say that the monster is the harbinger of crises — for Preciado, and for any other who seeks to explore absolute particularity, these crises must not be explained away. They must be lived, and every partisan must choose their side.

This is simply because capitalist ideology can never entirely destroy the monster; whether through Blochian non-synchronicity or the development of new disciplinary procedures and techniques, the monster will always return. As Preciado warns his audience: "Life is mutation and multiplicity. You need to understand that the future monsters are also your children and your grandchildren."[20] There is a recognition in this statement that the monster is not something to come; rather, the monster is always already here, a Blochian and utopian "Not-Yet" that exists under the skin, as it were, of capitalist modernity.[21] Preciado draws heavily on both Thomas Kuhn and Bruno Latour to discuss the necessity of what he calls epistemological insubordination. To be monstrous, a Gothic Marxist politics demands both the utilisation of the revolutionary tools and awareness of the new knowledge that a monstrous epistemology can bring into being. Toward the end of his speech — presumably the portion that could not be delivered in person before he was driven from the stage by a mob with flaming torches — Preciado offers a warning. The new monsters that psychoanalysis has sought to normalise within its discourses are also a warning: a warning of a "new necropolitical alliance between the colonial patriarchate and new pharmacopornographic technologies." In similar language, Judith Butler raises comparable concerns in a piece they wrote for the *Guardian*:

Gender comes to stand for, or is linked with, all kinds of imagined "infiltrations" of the national body — migrants, imports, the disruption of local economics through the effects of globalization. Thus "gender" becomes a phantom, sometimes specified as the "devil" itself, a pure force of destruction threatening God's creation (not, I gather, climate change, which would be a much more likely candidate). Such a phantasm of destructive power can only be subdued through desperate appeals to nationalism, anti-intellectualism, censorship, expulsion, and more strongly fortified borders. One reason, then, we need gender studies more than ever is to make sense of this reactionary movement.[22]

What is striking here is Butler's use of the language of haunting — of ghosts, evils, and the devil. Both Preciado and Butler, then, are advocating for a monstrous feminism as a necessary revolt against a necropolitics that seeks to both create and annihilate its own monsters. This necropolitical alliance is in the nation-building business, an attempt to secure and maintain the boundaries of capitalism that is itself necrotic and inescapably haunted. The monster points to an outside, to the horrifying potential that life need not be like this; thus, the monster is a reconfiguration of life struggling to come into being. To read the Gothic and monstrous within both politics and culture is to inevitably be drawn to the possibilities of that reconfiguration. Jones, in their aphorisms, refers to the monster as the spectre of its abolition, a sign that takes on itself the detritus of history to beckon the partisan toward the future. For Tom Moylan, it is not enough for us to simply think of utopia or to seek the utopian traces within the present situation; rather, there must be both a collective and an ontological shift, a breaking of the habitus of our current subjectivity in search of the new. After all, for Moylan — and for Preciado — utopia is not a place or a programme, it is a becoming.[23] As Preciado closes his plea to the psychoanalysts: "Join the monsters!"[24] This is the beginning of a Gothic Marxist politics.

CHAPTER SIX

GHOSTS AND THE HAUNTING OF MODERNITY

The previous chapter talked about the importance of monstrosity as a metaphor for the current political moment. As Paul Preciado points out, the discursive metaphor of monstrosity is useful and necessary in precisely the ways it allows for new modes of knowledge and new ways of life to find cogent expression. Another common metaphor that we have internalised at the current conjuncture of modernity is that of the cloud. This is an architectural and spatial metaphor that structures our contemporary relationship to technology and is absolutely ingrained in the realities of our day-to-day life. Computational and connected systems make up our shared social space, which increasingly comes to reflect that same set of technologies, being heavily privatised, capitalistic, and monitored by corporate power. In a sense, the internet is difficult to discuss — after all, one of the challenges for any mode of cultural analysis is to be aware of that which increasingly seems natural. The internet is in so many ways part of the very architecture not just of our social lives but of our worlds — all of culture is, as James Bridle puts it, a code/space, a geography enmeshed with the technologies of the digital age.[1] Bridle's book on the internet, *New Dark Age*, takes its title from a famous line from H. P. Lovecraft's short story "The Call of Cthulhu," which proposes a bleak vision of knowledge completely overwhelming human subjectivity. As the opening of the story puts it:

> The most merciful thing in the world, I think, is the inability of the human mind to correlate all its contents. We live on a placid island of ignorance in the midst of black seas of infinity, and it was not meant that we should voyage far. The sciences, each straining in its own direction, have hitherto harmed us little; but some day the piecing together of dissociated knowledge will open up such terrifying vistas of reality, and of our frightful position therein, that we shall either go mad from the revelation or flee from the deadly light into the peace and safety of a new dark age.[2]

We think of the internet as intangible — as a cloud — but it is a very carefully constructed, complex, and fundamentally concrete object. We are inside of it, perpetually — from our data being harvested and sold to advertisers, to facial recognition, to the computer banking services that process billions of credit card purchases, all the way up to the infrastructure that underpins the exploitation of the global stock market and the American war machine. A problem arises, of course, when two things start to happen: when the structure that we are within runs up against the limitations and antagonisms of capital, and when the sheer weight of accumulated history becomes too difficult to ignore. Preservation and history are difficult to maintain on the internet. From constant updates to every major website, to the more prosaic issue of link decay, the internet is both permanent, massively distributed, and at the same time phenomenally fragile. So much of the web just sits there now, no longer functional: links that are now piggybacked to spam, malware, or procedurally generated sludge, profiles on websites long abandoned, comment threads populated by faces and emptied of consciousness.

We're all haunted now — this is just a simple truth of our present age. On the mundane level, this is visible in the multiple selves and multiple versions of selves reflected and represented in our social media profiles. In the wake of the rise of platform capitalism and the ever-encroaching digitisation of our daily lives, we have inevitably and inexorably all become our own ghosts. This chapter offers an exploration of ghosts and spectrality in the age of the internet, moving across films like Kiyoshi Kurosawa's *Pulse* (2001) and *Unfriended: Dark Web* (2018) to Rob Savage's *Host* (2020). Our ever-increasing integration into the digital sphere doesn't just fracture the subject, but transforms it into a spectral presence that is rearticulated and performed in new ways across all of the platforms we are now tied to. This of course carries with it deep economic issues, as Wendy Liu's work on the necessity of the abolition of Silicon Valley has pointed out.[3] In our present age, the ghost is no longer simply an externality made visible but a reflection of our own deeply alienated states: just think of the ways in which platform capitalism, combined with the gig economy, has perfected the practice of alienation, reducing delivery drivers or cab drivers to nothing so much as avatars on a screen, rendering invisible their work and making labour organising increasingly difficult.[4] This, of course, is not just an existential problem; it can be linked to the liquidation of class consciousness under capitalist realism[5] and the increasing destabilisation of labour in total, highlighting the ways in which Gothic Marxism brings together individual philosophical and political struggles with a broader critique of capitalism as a system. As neoliberal precarity has brought more of not just our economic but our social life into the market — and of course, erased the distinction between those two things — o many of us have become spectres haunting the ruins of modernity itself.

Much of the early commercial internet was shaped by technological limitation; adoption of the technology was not widespread and was still undergoing the privatisation that moved much of the internet infrastructure out of the hands of governments and into the private sector.[6] As a result, access to the early-2000s internet was somewhat limited, requiring one either to have access to technology which was beyond the reach of the mass market, or to be affiliated with a research or educational institution. Naturally, then, network technology took some time to filter into the structure of feeling that is horror media. While there were some earlier, promising attempts — perhaps most notably David Cronenberg's *Videodrome* (1983) — generally it wasn't until the early 2000s that the internet became sufficiently well known to be of interest to horror film directors. The emergence of web technology required adaptation in order for its action to be integrated into the narrative structure of cinema. The Russian-Kazakh director and producer Timur Bekmambetov developed some of the first rules for what he termed the "screen movie." In a gesture reminiscent of the Dogme 95 movement, Bekmambetov sought to codify the ways in which technological expression was integrated cinematically. This included that screen movies needed to be made up entirely of computer screens, without camera movement; they should take place completely in real time; and the soundtrack should only include audio that occurs diegetically from within the computer. Obviously, there are plenty of films that bend or break these rules, but as Bekmambetov pointed out in an interview, this is simply an attempt to solve the problem of representing in film the truth of how people increasingly live — in a social world entirely mediated via screen technology.[7] It has also been argued that the screen film is just the latest iteration of the way in which film has always been enmeshed within wider media and technology ecosystems; using Shane Denson and Julia Leyda's term, we can consider the screen film, the VR film, or interactive film as a kind of "post-cinema."[8]

Generally, *The Collingswood Story* (2002) is regarded as the first true screen film, and it wasn't until the *Unfriended* films of the 2010s that the device was integrated authentically into a mainstream film release. Leaving aside the screen film style, another interesting strand of internet horror understood the internet as a tool for real-world interpersonal exploitation. This ties into the prevalent moral panic about young people and children accessing the internet, and the concomitant return of a "stranger danger" paranoia about the risks of faceless avatars in chat rooms and on IM services. While undoubtedly bound up within a reactionary and disciplinary "think of the children" moral anxiety, one of the most interesting and aesthetically successful of these early internet horror films was David Slade's *Hard Candy* (2005). This minimalist two-hander starring Elliot Page and Patrick Wilson examines the ways in which the internet can serve to facilitate child sexual exploitation and the ways in which networked technology allows for the exercise of a new kind of agency — pre-emptive revenge upon the predator. What is interesting about these films is the extent to which there is often very little by way of the supernatural; there's plenty of violence and, in many, the usual cinematic tricks that allow killers to move at seemingly superhuman speeds, but the horror is framed in essentially human terms. What this suggests is that, even from its earliest iterations, in the screen film or the internet horror film there was a profound awareness of the ways in which the increasing technological mediation of our social being would have a powerful estranging impact.

In this context, Kiyoshi Kurosawa's 2001 film *Pulse* becomes less an oddity or exception than an explicit consideration of the social alienation that the internet both accelerates and intensifies, as well as a reflection on the already existing economic contradictions of capitalism that the internet — as product and mode of production — cannot obscure or resolve. Emerging as one of the defining texts of the so-called Japanese lost decade, the film details what the ghost is in this particular age of technology. Following two parallel storylines and structured in a manner reminiscent of a dream, the film follows two groups of characters who start to realise that people are seeing ghosts on the internet and that these ghosts are having a profound impact on the real world. Michi and her colleagues (Junko Sasano, Toshio Yabe, and Taguchi) work at a flower delivery business; student Ryosuke Kawashima signs up for a new internet service provider and makes friends with a computer science student to help him make sense of the strange visions and messages he starts to receive.

Those involved start to seal off parts of their homes as forbidden zones, demarcated with red tape; later, they appear to their friends as alive when already dead (often by suicide), and the end of the film (arguably its weakest point, as the film begins to trade atmosphere for spectacle) sees an apocalyptic incursion of the dead into the world of the living. Its narrative construction and formal qualities echo its thematic ideas about loneliness and technology. The film itself appeared just before the "cloud" would begin taking over as the dominant metaphor for thinking about computation. The computers in *Pulse* have a kind of physicality that was slowly becoming obsolete: they require a phone line, and the screens are not the slick, invisibilised technology we are used to now; they take up space within the frame, making their function as the mediating object in interpersonal relationships impossible to ignore.

What is really notable about the film's philosophy of the internet is how it differs from a lot of other internet horror. For the most part, the internet was posited as a kind of externality — this thing that could be instrumentalised for nefarious actors or that could make its way into the so-called real world. However, in *Pulse*, the web is not an externality but an emerging internality of human subjectivity. One implication of this is the film's understanding that the internet is not a cause of the metaphysical alienation that the ghosts represent: the internet is simply a doorway. This way, we can start to understand the internet as something other than a mechanism for reproducing an already existing narcissism (the "black mirror" of modernity) and can begin to understand the internet as a cyberspace in which we navigate our own desires, social relationships, and our relationship to history itself.[9] To put this another way: if what was originally seen as the so-called real world has become a code/space, it's important to recognise the architecture and topography of the digital mansion within which we experience the world. Ghosts, space, and time: with these three aspects, *Pulse* is readable as a kind of haunted house film, a reflection of the haunted cyberspace in which we are all already enmeshed.

What this brings to the fore is the relationship between the living and the dead. Kurosawa, in an interview, highlighted that the ghosts of *Pulse* are not malicious or even really that hostile. His point is well worth quoting in full:

I find ghosts in Japanese horror much more terrifying. In the standard American Horror canon, because a ghost violently attacks you or comes after you, at least you have the chance to fight back. And what you're fighting for is the idea that you can beat the bad thing and go back to the good old days when you were peaceful and happy and there weren't any ghosts hanging around. But if they don't attack you then the best you can do is figure out a way to co-exist with them. I find the idea that one just has to live with this thing much more terrifying. You have no chances of running away or fighting it; you're stuck with it forever.[10]

The internet, then, is caught in the attempt to establish a constant present and at the same time haunted by the ruins over which the latest new thing is constructed. These ghosts are not hostile — they are us: lonely, atomised, and seeking connection. *Pulse* shares some common commitments to something like John Berger's "On the Economy of the Dead," which insists upon the common ground between the living and the dead and the importance of embracing that interdependency.[11] Any kind of haunting is also necessarily bound up with grief, and while *Pulse* emerges from a very specific cultural context relating to the shaping of Japanese society through the development of an American-led global capitalist hegemony, it is the universality of capitalist experience that allows the film to resonate so widely. There is something utopian at work here in Michi, who calls the ghost her friend, and even the very end of the film — in which the world comes to a spectral conclusion — is a world-ending event, but as Kurosawa puts it in the interview quoted above, the apocalyptic vision is in no way entirely "negative or despairing, it was positive, a way to get rid of old baggage."

Appearing just as the internet was adopted en masse, the film is surprisingly nuanced and hopeful about technology. If there is a horror in *Pulse*, it is loneliness, elevated to a metaphysics beyond simple existential malaise. For all the uncertainty, dread, and ambiguity that the new world of the internet offers, the film also thinks that ghosts are not something to be ignored or repressed. Rather, we have to recognise the potential within this new technology to bring us all into a strange new kind of intimacy, one that goes beyond our spatial reality and stretches beyond our atomisation and alienation — even through death itself. However, as technology continued to develop, becoming more and more a part of our social being, this potential for intimacy and solidarity revealed a flip side.

If in *Pulse* the source of fear and the bleak atmosphere is an endemic and near-universal loneliness finding new expression via technology, then in *Unfriended: Dark Web* (2018), what this same (albeit now more sophisticated) technology brings into the social world is both boredom and sadism. The film was produced and developed by Timur Bekmambetov and represents the mainstreaming of the screen film concept. The film follows Matias (Colin Woodell), an app developer, and his group of friends: Damon, AJ, Lexx, Serena, and Nari (played by Andrew Lees, Connor Del Rio, Savira Windyani, Rebecca Rittenhouse and Betty Gabriel). The group decide to have a game night through Skype, with technology providing a medium for their interaction and jokes during a game of Cards Against Humanity. Matias has acquired a new laptop, and in between keeping up with friends, he uses the laptop to work on an app that will live-translate his spoken words into ASL for his deaf girlfriend. Struggling for money, it turns out that Matias has stolen the laptop from a local cybercafe. After poking around the laptop's files, the group stumble across a host of snuff videos and the wider network of the dark web through which recorded sadism and violence are enacted, commodified, and distributed. Over the course of the evening, the apparent former owner begins sending strange messages. These escalate, and the friends are picked off one by one as it's revealed that the whole situation was a set up: the laptop was planted and the whole series of events unfolded as a means for the shadowy group (within which each individual names themselves Charon) to find some convenient scapegoats to avoid culpability.

The film is an object lesson in the ways in which contemporary network technology produces both immediacy and culpability. In *Pulse*, cyberspace is represented but requires traversal and has a clear, identifiable kind of topography — the forbidden room. Accessing the internet is not something straightforward; it requires dedicated equipment or specialist knowledge. But in the space of just a decade or so, this radically shifted. In *Unfriended*, the space of cyberspace has collapsed: everything is immediate, accessible, and always already at hand. Matias moves from Facebook to the dark web almost seamlessly, reflecting the ways in which users have become more familiar with certain kinds of technology, and how technology has been designed for both ease of use and mass adoption, as well as inculcating a sense of paranoia that, even in the most familiar and banal of settings, violence is just a click or two away.

In an even more explicit example of this collapse of space,

one of the friends — Damon — is based in the UK, while the rest of the group live in the USA. When the group work out just what is going on and the extent of the danger they are all in, Damon is believed to be safe. The immediacy of cyberspace not only allows Damon to download the incriminating files but — of course — also allows one of the Charon group to break into Damon's home, hang him, and write a suicide note to complete the frame job. In effect, *Unfriended: Dark Web* underscores how the distinction between the real world and the haunted digital world — which *Pulse* posits — no longer exists. As Jing Yang argues, films like *Unfriended* "resemble the computer window interfaces characterized by hyperlink, decentralization and fragmentation, which reflects and will further cultivate spectators' screen life and Internet thinking in the real world."[12] However, this line of argument doesn't go quite far enough: after all, with so much of the physical infrastructure of modernity bound up within the digital, any demarcation ultimately collapses. Serena's mother is on life support, and her fiancée Nari leaves to travel via the subway to find the police. The Charons hack into the CCTV cameras at both the subway and the hospital and tell Serena that she has to choose who will live and who one will die. Unable to make the choice, both Serena's mother and Nari are killed within seconds of each other.

Perhaps the best example of how the film documents the collapse between the offline and online is the manner in which the Charons deal with AJ. He's an internet native, political in a meme-based way, making references to the Illuminati and the dangers of mega-corporations. He hosts his own webshow, "The Way of AJ," which concerns itself with Alex Jones-style rants about corruption, the beauty of the Second Amendment, and the importance of digital security.

There's a degree to which AJ represents a kind of political throwback — his vaguely leftish techno-libertarianism is a decade or so out of date and feels more like a reference to Obama-era politics — but his own paranoia is planted early in the film to induce a false sense of security. When the Charons turn their attention to AJ, he goads them, confident in his own cyber-security. Simply by using publicly available information and audio from his many live streams, the group are able arrange for AJ to be SWAT-ed. The group call 911, and using audio manipulation, issue threats that AJ is about to conduct a mass shooting. The SWAT team arrive and shoot AJ to death when the Charons play audio of what sounds like a gun cocking in order to provoke the police officers. It is a perfect "remote" murder — physical space collapsed into immediacy through the mediation of the internet, which is then turned back upon us to become an inescapable digital panopticon. To put this in the parlance of the internet, one can't simply log off — in fact, as the film details, to do so puts you at risk. You may have logged off, but you are still observable, and even behind a keyboard, you can never consider yourself safe.

Toward the end of the film, a desperate Matias asks the Charons why they are doing this. The answer is simple and obvious: for entertainment. Back in 2015, the journalist Patrick Klepek conducted an interview with a SWAT-er (an online troll who arranges for targets to be harassed or arrested by armed police), whose rationalisation of their behaviour was exactly the same. To quote them directly, being "able to intimidate someone is really fun, whether someone will admit it or not."[13] To put this another way, the collapse of cyberspace into an omnipresent immediacy has made the internet boring and therefore sadistic — what else is there to do other than transgress? There's a degree of necessary depersonalisation involved here: those who enjoy SWAT-ing others, or who enjoy trolling and abuse, can't really think of their targets as "real" people; they become less than human, and there is arguably a sense of power in using a computer to make changes in the physical world. This raises the problem of guilt and complicity, or to put it back into the language of the Gothic, the problem of haunting. After all, the ethical problem here is not resolved through legislative punishment for technologically mediated sadism, nor can it be hand-waved away through performative moral injunctions to "just be kind" online. What we have to recognise is that the internet has fundamentally changed the means by which subjectivity finds expression. Social beings have been networked together through the monopolistic enclosure of the digital commons. We are all always together, always reminded of our past — no post is ever truly gone, after all — and as a result, we are always bored. The philosopher Nolen Gertz argued that technology wouldn't take away our freedom but that we would willingly give it up — free ourselves of the existential burden of free will by outsourcing it to the algorithm (which already decides what we watch and what we might enjoy from Amazon). Technology has numbed us, trapped us within anhedonic feedback loops in which "the technology used for distracting us from our sufferings become technologies used for inflicting suffering on the world."[14]

Yet, it is easy to retort that sometimes reliance on technology becomes a necessity. During the height of the COVID-19 pandemic, there were widespread lockdowns across the world. The internet became the primary means by which large sections of the global workforce could be kept in work,[15] and through which countless social relationships could be maintained. This was, of course, great business for countless technology companies. The biggest winner was probably the video conferencing tool Zoom, which announced year-on-year profit growth of over 300 percent between 2020 and 2021.[16] In terms of horror cinema, the period of lockdown presented both a serious challenge and an opportunity.

In 2020, the streaming platform Shudder released *Host*, directed by Rob Savage. In many ways, it is the high point of the formal and technological development of the screen film, taking place entirely on a Zoom call. The film was produced and directly entirely remotely too, in keeping with UK lockdown laws, and it depends heavily on practical effects that the actors rigged and executed without a larger production team. Thus, it serves as both an implementation of the points made by Timur Bekmambetov and a record of a specific moment in UK cultural history.

What is immediately striking about the film, in comparison to *Unfriended*, is the insight it provides into internet sociology. *Unfriended* presents a younger demographic: they meet via Skype — if the film were made today, it's easy to see it happening through a Discord server — and each of them has an identifiable relationship to technology and an accompanying aesthetics. AJ and Damon, in particular, are clear digital natives ("terminally online," to use the appropriate Twitter-slang) with a fondness for technology and the seemingly obligatory neon strip-lighting to make the technology look as cool as possible.

In contrast, everything in *Host* happens through Zoom. From the outset, this immediately positions the film within a specific demographic: if the friends in *Unfriended* were in their late teens to mid-twenties, the fact that *Host* utilises a Zoom call identifies the characters as both more professional and significantly older. They all clearly went to university together — they're a group of former university friends who all moved to London and decide to hangout via Zoom to help themselves through their middle-class lockdown boredom. In order to add some excitement to their time together, Haley (Haley Bishop) has hired a medium, Seylan (Seylan Baxter), to organise a virtual séance. Of course, something goes wrong, and the group manage to summon a tulpa or demonic spirit; over the course of the rest of the film, they are progressively haunted and killed in a variety of ways.

Rob Savage developed the film into a full-length feature after a Zoom-based prank he recorded went viral and he was contacted by producers. The plot itself is remarkably derivative of earlier films — the *Unfriended* films and *The Blair Witch Project* are heavy points of reference — but what's most important about the film is its metatextual conversation regarding the ways in which technology met the biopolitical problem of COVID. With the major wave of lockdowns receding into memory, *Host* is a great record of how the creative and middle classes felt throughout the lockdown and of the resulting anxieties and neurosis this brought about.

The theoretical and critical writing that emerged immediately during or just after the height of COVID represents something of a mixed bag. Most (in)famous perhaps is the biopolitical panic of Giorgio Agamben, who compared lockdowns in Italy to the fascism of Nazi Germany — a point so inflammatory that even one of his own translators sought to distance himself from Agamben as a thinker.[17] While there is inarguably some degree of truth to the idea that the lockdowns and other biopolitical moves were designed to weaponize a crisis of health, such moves can't be considered in separation from the drive within capitalism to maintain and perpetuate accumulation. You might not be able to go to work any more, but you can certainly still work remotely. In contrast, Franco Berardi's *The Third Unconscious* was also written during lockdown and represents a less intellectually rigid approach to the problem. For Berardi, the pandemic represented the return of death to the centre of discourse — after all, what is death if not the great limit that capitalism cannot overcome. We cannot be together, because that equals death in the era of lockdown, as even the virtual sociality of *Host* proves. We could be together apart, but even that virtual togetherness does not nullify the threat. If the horror of *Pulse* was loneliness, and that of *Unfriended* was sadistic boredom, then in *Host* the horror is in the suspension of real life and the inseparability of death from the realm of the social, however it might be mediated.

Berardi puts the problem like this:

> Real life is now this: burning forests, melting ices, air pollution, pandemics. Therefore real life is replaced by digital networking and bodily conjunction is replaced by machine connection… Bios has broken the chain of techno-linguistic automatisms and is now revealing the horizon of extinction…[18]

What did we want during lockdown? We wanted to escape the real world and to be reminded of the world which had been taken away by the virus. Yet, even here, in the lockdown, wherein the rules of normality were suspended (at least for some), the mediating structure of technology did not solve the problem of invisible presence — it might have kept out the virus, but it could not keep out the supernatural. For Berardi, lockdown and the pandemic represented chaos: a moment when the rules and standard expectations of capitalism were suspended and the future remained a kind of open question. In retrospect, it's easy to dismiss Berardi for his naivety, but while lockdown did disrupt the chains of automation that capitalism had operated along, there were also new, more widely adopted technological tools — Zoom being perhaps the most immediately obvious. The internet as a Gothic space — one redolent with ghosts, spirits, or other hauntings — is not just a metaphor. In the context of *Host*, it reflects a sense of loss — the loss of "the normal," to which so much of capitalist politics has been trying to get back for years now. However, Berardi raises an important utopian point: "Time is suspended and we don't know what will happen next. A return to the old normalcy? A comeback of the inflection? Death? A famous slogan of 1968: *Cours camarade, le vieux monde est derrière toi!* (Run comrades, the old world is behind you!)."[19]

A haunting is a figure of a loss — of something missing; a lack, even (perhaps especially) — mediated through technology. Yet, if the old world is still with us, then the spectres of the past also raise the possibility not of going back to the old but of going forward into something new.

CHAPTER SEVEN

CRISES OF LIBERALISM AND NECRO-NEOLIBERALISM

One of the key aspects of contemporary horror — particularly in the mainstream of Hollywood cinema — has been its turn to the political over the past decade or so. This chapter analyses two of the most important franchises in contemporary American horror cinema, the Purge and Saw franchises. In their depictions of America's contemporary situation, the two franchises function as vicious satires of the real state of things. In their excess of horror, we see a twisted reflection of American liberalism and its collapse into violence and decay. The Saw franchise, marked by urban deindustrialisation, exploitative healthcare systems, and a biopolitics that sees life as commodity rather than a social mode of being, is the mirror of the Purge films, a franchise that recognises the ways in which capitalism functions but which is fundamentally unable to think outside of the antinomies of liberal ideology. In the Purge films, the capitalist state functions as the driver and instigator of a kind of Hobbesian violence whereby the exploited are forced to fend for themselves. Yet both franchises are trapped, with their critique suspended amid massively commercial horror. In the midst of this contradiction, the political valences of the films become clearer, showing us the darkest sides of contemporary politics — a catastrophe rotting away at the heart of American modernity.

Of the two franchises, the Saw films are perhaps the more notorious: the franchise started in 2004 and has grossed more than a billion dollars over the course of ten films and multiple games.[1] The films combine a grimy nu-metal aesthetic with practical effects and an approach to gore that both appeals to fans of extreme horror and provokes regular moral panic from conservative and establishment media. The film series originated in the creative partnership of James Wan and Leigh Whannell (both of whom have gone on to largely successful careers in mainstream cinema). The first film, *Saw* (2004), was made after the pair produced a short film about two men locked in a single room. It was shot on a budget of around one million dollars, and grossed over one hundred million at the box office. The premise is that the two characters, played by Cary Elwes and Whannel, have been kidnapped by the "Jigsaw Killer," a former engineer called John Kramer (played by veteran character actor Tobin Bell). Jigsaw places various victims into traps or games in order to test the victims' will to survive and the degree to which they value their lives: if they fail the test, the victim meets a spectacularly bloody end; pass, and they are supposedly transformed. At one point, Kramer even boasts that his methods are 100 percent effective and guarantee no chance of recidivism.

The first film is a competently made and quite brutally effective horror film, but from the outset the ideological commitments of the film are already somewhat strained. The largest problem — and it's one that the franchise has found almost impossible to solve — is that of "value." What does it mean to value one's life? From the outset, many of

Jigsaw's victims are suffering with mental health issues, substance abuse, and addiction, or are involved in low-level types of petty crime. Indeed, in later films, it turns out that many of the victims are taken from a free clinic set up by John Kramer's ex-wife, Jill. For the Jigsaw Killer, value — or the lack thereof — is an entirely moral failing that demands some retributive penalty, a particularly literal "pound of flesh" that has to be paid. In the moral economics of the films, things like depression, suicidal ideation, and self-harm reflect a failure to value life on an individual level, but in the lifeworld of the films, there is no wider social totality — all that exists are individuals to be made into test subjects and largely ineffective law enforcement. This conception of human subjectivity is profoundly neoliberal, exemplifying what Mark Fisher referred to as responsibilisation: a state of politics in which systemic issues become something for which the individual has to take responsibility — and of course, because the individual cannot solve the issues, they can be blamed for their failures, which can serve as a means to excuse the society that produces these systemic problems. Thus, the films both demonise and punish the poor, the addicts, and the petty criminals for moral failings, turning their punishment into spectacular displays of gore and violence.

In short, the Saw franchise exists to make a spectacle of the neoliberal exercise of sovereignty over the bodies of those who are made expendable by virtue of their perceived failures in the moral economy of the film world. The Saw films echo the argument of Cameroonian political theorist and historian Achille Mbembe, who discusses the particular kind of power that operates in colonial contexts — a targeted, ruthless biopower Mbembe calls "necropolitics." Mbembe's rightly famous essay opens as follows: "The ultimate expression of sovereignty resides, to a large degree, in the power and the capacity to dictate who may live and who must die. Hence, to kill or to allow to live constitute the limits of sovereignty."[2] The resonances of this with the Saw films are abundantly clear — one only need think of Jigsaw's famous slogan/instruction to those enmeshed within his games, a line delivered often through the infamous figure of Billy the Puppet: "Live or die, make your choice."

Mbembe's point, of course, builds on three other important sources: Michel Foucault remains one the prime theorists of sovereignty, alongside Giorgio Agamben, but it is the Nazi jurist Carl Schmitt who provided the foundational formulation of the term in the opening line of his book, *Political Theology*: "Sovereign is he who decides on the exception."[3] Agamben, in his own work, would map this state of exception in a series of pathbreaking analyses of the political institutions of the West. For Agamben, it was in the Nazi camps that sovereignty "acquire[d] a permanent spatial arrangement that remains continually outside the normal state of law."[4] He expanded his analysis of the state of exception in the wake of the war on terror, a political set of mechanisms that allows governments to make the suspension of the rule of law the norm, and places those deemed to be enemies outside of any normative mechanism of justice. Think of the inhabitants of Guantanamo Bay, many of whom will die in confinement or have already passed away without ever being charged. Detainees at Guantanamo have vanished into a vicious and inescapable topology: the global network of CIA prisons and torture sites. The first three films of the Saw franchise, in particular, all embody this idea: set predominately in abandoned warehouses, derelict industrial estates, or abattoirs, the settings literalise this point, placing the characters in specific spatial configurations outside of the juridical structures of the norm. The third film in the franchise made these themes most explicit, which would be the main concern of the franchise from that point on.

Saw III (2006) marks the point at which the films give up on the idea of the games having any element of fairness (one of the characters even reveals that the games are now impossible to win and the traps are designed to be inescapable. Unsurprisingly, she too later ends up in a trap from which she cannot escape). The film's plot becomes increasingly complex over time as the franchise introduces more characters and has to explain how John Kramer can accomplish all that he does without snapping narrative believability. Thus, *Saw III* follows two main story lines. Firstly, there are the experiences of Lynn (Bahar Soomekh), a doctor who is kidnapped in order to take care of John Kramer, who is dying from a terminal brain tumour. Lynn is monitored by one of John's acolytes, Amanda (played by Shawnee Smith), a former drug addict who survived the infamous reverse bear trap from the first film. The second story line follows Jeff, a depressed, deeply angry man grieving the loss of his son, who was killed in a drunk-driving accident. Jeff is put into situations where he must choose whether to allow those involved in the case (the witness, the judge, and the perpetrator) to die, or risk bodily injury to save them. At first, Jeff allows the people in question to suffer, before — unsuccessfully — trying to save them. Ultimately, the two stories intersect: Lynn is revealed to be Jeff's wife; the games are designed to test Jeff's potential capacity for forgiveness; and Amanda is being tested to see if she can follow through on what the film argues is John Kramer's philosophy of violence. The narrative collapses into disaster as John, Amanda, Jeff, and Lynn all end up dead.

There are a couple of important things about the film that underscore the degree to which it is concerned with a particular kind of biopolitical sovereignty. Jeff's emotional, grief-stricken response to the death of his son is completely reasonable, yet it is presented as a sign of some kind of moral failing: his depression and the social consequences of it are what attract Jigsaw's attention. The traps that the victims are placed in are some of the franchise's most explicit, and Jeff clearly takes a libidinal pleasure in watching their suffering. The biopolitical structures of the Saw franchise, and of Jigsaw's wider philosophy, are (as discussed) highly neoliberal, and at their core, are essentially retributive. The franchise is often labelled as a kind of torture porn, but this misses the emotional tonality and affect that the retributive action of the plot aims at: the films are not aiming for the mimetic realism of pornography, but the melodrama and abstraction of a soap opera. The films are orthogonal to cinematic realism, but — like many soap operas and melodramas — they tend to be more ideologically transparent in their commitments.

The first three films are, in essence, an example of what we might term a necro-neoliberalism, representing the point at which the necropolitical strategies of sovereignty perfected in American colonialism return back to the imperial core. America, deindustrialised, is presented as a vast swathe of rain-soaked streets, muted colours, and industrial decay; the population base, suffering immense social deprivation and the annihilation of class consciousness, is essentially surplus to requirements, functioning only as always-already-guilty victims or incompetent law enforcement officers. Here, then, the film's biopolitics is neoliberal in its moralism and individualisation, but also necrotic, taking its unwilling victims to the very limit of bare life, making the "pound of flesh" horrifyingly literal. The gore of the films is, in a sense, about the surplus of the body — how much of yourself are you willing to lose to continue your life? To put this another way, the Saw films enact our fundamental disposability under the constraints of American neoliberal, biopolitical sovereignty.

However, after *Saw III*, the later films underwent a shift, and even made an attempt at some measure of social criticism and engagement, but they could never articulate anything outside of the necro-neoliberal political frame. The principal crimes for which people in the franchise are punished — when these rise above drug addiction and mental health issues — generally revolve around property development and speculation. The main trap sequence of *Saw V* includes people who were involved in causing an apartment fire that killed eight others, and this reflects a broader awareness of the degree to which the American economy is principally a FIRE economy (financial, insurance, and real estate), as productive labour has been outsourced overseas, particularly in the aftermath of the decline of US unions from the 1970s onward, and legislation like NAFTA in the mid-1990s. In fact, the entire conceit of *Saw V*'s central trap sequence underscores the extent to which the action is determined by this necro-neoliberalism. The sequence follows five people, placing them in a variety of traps; the group come to believe that the only way they can survive is by killing off one of their fellow victims. It is entirely a zero-sum game: for me to live, you have to die. The final trap reveals that, equally as they were all complicit, all could have survived — the zero-sum game of neoliberalism has been so internalised that it is impossible to view others as anything other than a threat.

It's *Saw VI* that represents the franchise's clearest attempt to articulate some kind of criticism of necro-neoliberalism, but the film can ultimately only compulsively restage it. In the wake of the election of Barack Obama, one of the primary debates in mainstream US politics was over healthcare. The same year *Saw VI* was released, the media was overtaken by debates about the ACA (the Affordable Care Act, Obama's landmark attempt to reform the bloated necropolitical institution of for-profit healthcare). *Saw VI* addresses the issue head on through its engagement with John Kramer's terminal cancer. In one of many interminable flashbacks, we see Kramer confront a health-insurance executive, William Easton (Peter Outerbridge). Kramer has his insurance coverage denied due to the machinations of the insurance company's probability algorithm. John's response to the news is as follows:

> Politicians, they say the same thing, over and over and over again. "Healthcare decisions should be made by doctors and their patients, not by the government." Well, now I know they're not made by doctors and their patients or the government. They're made by the fuckin' insurance companies.

Saw VI, then, recognises the necro-neoliberalism of the American FIRE economy and the ways in which the individual is rendered a disposable asset class ("Can you afford to stay alive?" is the dominate question of both the American healthcare system and all of the Saw films), yet Kramer's response exemplifies the ways in which the films are both a comment on and product of that same necro-neoliberal model. For Kramer, what the insurance company misses is a kind of neoliberal vitalism — no algorithm can account for the drive to live that is innate within the subject. As a result, Easton is placed into a variety of games involving those he works alongside. Yet again, the film lapses into an easy moralism. For example, someone who smokes ends up having their lungs crushed; a fate they apparently deserve because they chose to keep smoking, despite being at risk.

The central trap mechanic of the film is perhaps the most impactful trap in the whole series: the carousel. William is confronted by six of his associates, who are strapped to a carousel with a shotgun pointing at their chests. As the device spins, William is forced to choose who will be in the firing line when the gun goes off, and he can only save two out of the six associates. The message left for William is well worth reproducing in full, highlighting the ways in which it is the exercise of sovereignty that most concerns the films:

> Hello, William. Before you are six of your most valuable associates. The ones who find errors in policies. Their findings result in over two-thirds of all applications denied or prematurely terminated. Now you must apply your analysis to them. And will you be able to find their errors? Six ride the carousel — but only two can get off. The decision of which two survive falls upon you. But remember: the mounted gun will continue to fire until all six rounds are spent. And if no decision is made on your part, all six will perish. To offer the two reprieves, you must press both buttons at once in the box before you. However, in doing so, you will give a sacrifice of your own. Two can live, four will die, your decisions symbolized by the blood on your hands.

The film then forces a confrontation with the violent neoliberal individualisation of society, but it can only do so in individualist terms — the issue, of course, is not that this one person has chosen to work for an insurance company; the issue the film grasps indirectly is that a system of for-profit healthcare sees human contingency, fragility, and sickness as fundamentally economic failings, rather than as inescapable aspects of our shared and common humanity. Unsurprisingly, then, the film — right at the end — lapses back into retributive and violent moral punishment. Easton is confronted by the family of a man he denied healthcare to, and they are given the choice of whether to free him or inject his body with strong acid, dissolving him into abject flesh. What's truly grim about the ending is that it is the son of the man whose care was denied that eagerly enacts vengeance, as if the systemic injustices of the US healthcare system and the all-too-human grief of the encounter with bodily finitude can be rectified through turning one bad actor into sludge. The true horror of the franchise is not in the individual spectacle of violence, but in the wider architecture that makes it both inescapable and something all are willing to enact whenever the opportunity presents itself.

For a more sustained engagement with the realities of American necro-neoliberal biopower, the Purge franchise — which in many ways succeeded and exceeds the Saw films — offers more possibilities for horror to function as a diagnosis of the current conjunction (even if, ultimately, the films cannot go beyond a kind of liberal American exceptionalism). The Purge franchise consists of five films produced between 2013 and 2021, and two seasons of a television show[5] made between 2018 and 2020. The franchise emerged after the Saw franchise dropped in popularity and is set in a near-future America under a Christo-fascist political regime called the New Founding Fathers. As an antidote to social problems, the government introduces a twelve-hour overnight period, occurring once a year, during which all crime is legal. The night is supposed to allow for participants to express their negativity, anger, and libidinal desire for violence — this is the titular "purge." Like the methods of Kramer in the Saw franchise, the New Founding Fathers claim extraordinary levels of efficacy for the purge: at the beginning of *The Purge* (2013), the United States is apparently almost crime free, and its unemployment rate is less than 1 percent.

The first film follows James Sandin and his family as they attempt to make it through the night of the Purge. Sandin, played by Ethan Hawke, makes his living working for a company that manufactures home security systems, and he lives with his family in an exclusive gated community in Los Angeles. During the course of the evening, while watching the home security monitors, Sandin's son, Charlie (Max Burkholder), sees a wounded black man (played by Edwin Hodge) begging for help and temporarily disables the security systems to allow the man inside. The house is then surrounded by a group of armed and masked purgers who demand that Sandin hand over the stranger to be tortured and murdered. Sandin refuses, and the family is forced to defend the house as the masked intruders break in. Sandin dies in the course of the attack, and with the help of the bloodied stranger and the Sandins' neighbours, the group of invaders are killed. However, the final twist of the film is that the neighbours are not acting out of altruism or some sense of community solidarity, but out of envy: they want to kill the Sandins themselves. The root of their envy is the Sandins' economic position. The neighbours hate the Sandin family because their wealth is built off home security systems. As the film ends, Mary Sandin (Lena Headey) smashes her neighbour in the face with a shotgun and tells them that they will wait out the rest of the purge peacefully.

From the outset, there are two sets of class antagonisms within the film, which subsequent entries in the franchise both return to and refine. Firstly, there is the relationship between the bloodied stranger, the purgers, and the Sandin family. The bloody stranger is not given a name and is a homeless black man in the middle of a gated, predominantly white community in LA. The masked purgers address the Sandins as class equals, referring to the stranger as a swine, fit only for murder. The relationship between the economically wealthy and the poor is annihilationist: an asymmetrical class war naturalised through the overarching ontology of innate violence that the films see as being universal and inescapable. The second element of class antagonism is framed through envy. The intraclass antagonism of the rich is a product of the complete collapse of American class consciousness, and once again reinscribes the position that survival or success is only achievable at the cost of the other. Class, in a sense, becomes the vanishing mediator needed to make sense of the themes that the films are trying to develop. Rather than confront both class and capitalism directly, the first film's heavy-handed use of American symbolism (exemplified by the almost parodic use of "America, the beautiful" in the trailer) shows that its critique of American society is framed in the same moralistic rhetoric of late-Obama-era liberalism. In other words, the material quality and nature of economic injustice, racialised capitalism, and housing inequality are buried beneath a wave of American symbolism that refuses any serious engagement with the material basis of violence. This isn't to say that the kind of interpersonal violence the films deal with is unrealistic, or to lapse into a model of human subjectivity that sees this kind of behaviour as completely alien, but rather to insist upon the fact that this kind of anger, hatred, and violence is always rooted in material causes. Social antagonism is socially mediated and doesn't simply spring into existence from some essential human nature that has to be regularly purged. What makes this particularly frustrating is that the first three films in the franchise all take place in LA — a city that, as the late great Mike Davis pointed out, quite literally concretises issues of racial segregation, historical redlining, and violence into its very geography, and all these historically and socially mediated issues form the unacknowledged background of the violence that the entire franchise focuses on.[6]

Scholarship on the films has generally seen the franchise as proving that mainstream horror films in the 2010s could be both financially successful and political,[7] and while this is true, it's difficult to see the first film as political in any real sense of the term. Instead, it lapses into essentialist and non-materialist arguments that obscure the political critique the films seem to be aiming for. After all, its violence is simply emergent and extreme class envy among a racially homogenous middle class. Yet the second and third films in the series — *The Purge: Anarchy* (2014) and *The Purge: Election Year* (2016) — do deepen the franchise's political engagement. Both of these films expand on the thematics of the first, introducing a wider array of characters, making the sociological antagonisms even more heavy-handed, and introducing an anti-Purge (and even potentially revolutionary) movement. Spatially, the action also shifts away from the predominately white and wealthy gated communities of LA into the poorer, predominantly non-white communities of the high-rises and apartments of downtown. Perhaps the biggest shift from the first film is the introduction of an oppositional force to the New Founding Fathers led by Carmelo Jones (played by Michael K. Williams). Jones and the wider anti-Purge movement is (on the level of aesthetics) entirely indebted to the cultural legacy of radical movements such as the Black Panther Party in the American pop-culture imagination. From his shades, beret, AK-47, and radical broadcasts to the movement's mutual-aid and self-defence forces, Jones and the anti-Purge movement (which is predominately made up of working-class, non-white characters) have the potential to reintroduce an actual, explicit class conflict, to render the class war of the Purge no longer an asymmetrical fight. However, there are two problems these two films run into: the first is a sidelining of the black radical struggle; and the second is a lapse into liberal electoralism and a refusal to raise the hard question of revolutionary violence as a tactic within the broader issue of class war.

To offer a necessary gloss on the plot, the second film follows Leo Barnes (Frank Grillo), an off-duty LAPD sergeant who is looking for revenge against the person who killed his son and got off on a technicality (the parallels with *Saw III* here are difficult to ignore, both on the level of plot and theme). Barnes encounters a group of disparate figures stranded outside on the night of the Purge, and in the course of the film's events, discovers that the rich are paying for poor and working-class people to be abducted in order to ritualistically hunt them for sport. He does eventually find the man who killed his son, but learns to forgive, instead sparing him at the very last minute. This rather trite emotional journey is the key to the narrative of *The Purge: Election Year* (2016), in which Leo Barnes returns, now acting as the head of security for an anti-Purge presidential candidate, Charlie Roan (Elizabeth Mitchell). On the night of the purge, the New Founding Fathers revoke the immunity of government officials and try to have Roan assassinated by white supremacist militia forces. Roan and Barnes wind up on the streets of LA, and once again end up with a group of working-class individuals struggling to survive.

What this film makes explicit is that the Purge is an instrument of Malthusian population control: it's designed to kill off the poor in high numbers in order to reduce the economic burden on the state — an annihilationist intensification of already existing tendencies, but even with this as context, *Election Year* still refuses the possibility of revolutionary transformation. Roan and the various individuals who rescue her and Barnes once again come into contact with the anti-Purge movement, led by Dante Bishop (Edwin Hodge). The anti-Purge movement is planning to assassinate the leader of the New Founding Fathers, in a move that finds its echo in the Red Army Faction in Germany, the Red Brigades in the Italian Years of Lead, and countless other revolutionary movements that took seriously the question of revolutionary violence. In fact, the film takes time to disclose that the anti-Purge faction is even better resourced and organised than these real-world antecedents, with a well-established and extensive mutual-aid network and cadres of well drilled and heavily armed militants.

Roan is captured by New Founding Fathers forces, who intend to use her as a sacrifice in the midnight Purge mass that party apparatchiks take part in every year. For the New Founding Fathers, the Purge is fundamentally theological, involving a communion with the divine, intangible violence that is constitutive of American national self-identity. Again, while this comes close to a political critique of the theological justifications of American racial capitalism, slavery, and imperialism, it is also completely dehistoricised, making American violence out to be some protean and inevitable force. The anti-Purge militants, along with Leo Barnes, rescue Roan and capture the leadership of the New Founding Fathers. Yet here, Roan intervenes, imploring Bishop and his followers not to go through with his murder. The film literalises the struggle between emancipation through "any means necessary"[8] and a non-material, idealist and deeply ideological faith in the institutions of American democracy. At one point, Roan even invokes the "better angels of our nature," a Panglossian liberal and equally theological response to a theocratic government willing to use violence and possessing a seemingly endless supply of highly armed neo-Nazi militia members on speed dial. Roan — whose entire family was tortured to death in front of her during a Purge when she was a child — believes the only acceptable answer to the violence of New Founding Fathers is to vote *for her.*

The second and third films in the series fall into the same pattern as the first, identifying a crisis, and once again refusing to go beyond the conditions that instantiated the crisis in the first place. What is frustrating is that there are brief glimpses of more interesting political questions: the third film opens with murder tourism; Europeans coming to America specifically to purge. One of the characters, Joe, who owns a local deli, ends up having their Purge insurance premiums dramatically increased, yet all these political concerns are sublated into the figure of the good liberal technocrat.

The fourth film attempts something more sociologically interesting. This film, *The First Purge* (2018), looks at the initial Purge, run as a sociological experiment on Staten Island, among a poor black community in the projects. Participants are offered five thousand dollars to stay during the Purge, with the promise of more if they "participate". Here, the film comes closest to a kind of materialist grounding that might explain what causes the social antagonisms that need to be purged:

poverty, over-policing, and the exploitations of capitalism are all things the residents of the projects are *right* to feel angry about. The film follows Nya (Lex Scott Davis), a local activist, and Dmitri (Y'lan Noel), a local drug dealer, both of whom end up trapped on the island when the Purge is announced. Yet again, there is some heavy-handed moralism at play — when offered safety from the Purge by Dimitri, Nya responds by telling him that, while this Purge may represent a destructive force, "you destroy this community 364 days a year." Yet, it's Dimitri who ends up saving the community, rallying his troops to drive out the New Founding Fathers. In a moment when the film jettisons all subtlety, the New Founding Fathers are alarmed at the extent to which the poor black neighbourhoods don't seem to want to engage with the Purge, so KKK mobs are sent into these neighbourhoods to enact violence.

If the fourth film in the franchise is useful for anything, it's for documenting the franchises failure to move beyond its political horizons to look at the issues that the Purge aims to "solve." What is interesting is the extent to which gangs become an alternative to both the NFFA and emancipatory or revolutionary movements featured earlier in the franchise. If the third film shows liberal electoralism winning out over a black-led, working-class revolutionary movement, reflecting the concerted effort to fracture, imprison, and murder black radicals — again, something Mike Davis documented extensively in the context of LA specifically — then the fourth film highlights a point made by Fredric Jameson in one his most controversial works. Jameson's *An American Utopia* explores the collapse of dual-power movements and suggests that "maybe we should conclude that in this society it is in fact the Mafia [and gangs like them] which offers the most suggestive example of already existing dual power."[9] The concept of dual power comes from the Leninist idea of establishing an alternative to weak governmental power. In the context of the Purge franchise, it's quite arguable that the foundational role and purpose of the state is to allow people to live safely. In this case, the state is actively hostile to ordinary people, and so it's Dimitri's gang that secures the projects, serving as a de facto citizens' militia that drives out the KKK mercenaries who are threatening the community. In the third film, there is a key moment when the group are being tracked by armed militants and are rescued by the Crips. Again, to quote Jameson: "Perhaps the emergence of gangs and the drug trade is a symptom and a compensation for institutional weakness."[10] This institutional weakness functions as the background for the fifth — and so far final — film of the franchise, with its depiction of a terminal collapse in American society. Yet, it is in these brief moments that we can perhaps read the franchise against itself, pushing beyond the moralism of liberal-capitalist Hollywood. Throughout the second and third films, there are groups aiming for autonomous organisation, self-defence, and militancy, and who have a specific materialist understanding of why the state-sanctioned violence of the Purge night is really happening. As a model of resistance, the first film offers the nuclear family — revealed at the close to be rife with envy and violence, inextricably linked as it is with the foundations of capitalist modernity more generally. The anti-Purge movement incorporates the unhoused and the poor, and constructs a racially diverse militant force that takes seriously the point Lenin made — that revolutions are about state power.[11] If there is a future beyond the nightmare of violence that constitutes American capitalism, then the anti-Purge movement shows how that might be brought about. But as demonstrated in the *Purge* franchise, the contradiction between the revolutionary new and the *refusal* of revolutionary possibilities seems impossible to maintain. Rather than continue to develop this idea of almost destituent communism — wherein our power is not in our *authority* but precisely in our *capacity*[12] — and work toward a revolution that would not depose but replace the fascist-theocratic sovereigns of the New Founding Fathers, the fifth film in the series jettisons the utopian potential of revolution for a franchise conclusion that is both bleak and annihilationist.

Of all the films in the franchise, *The Forever Purge* most explicitly grounds itself in the real-world social context, particularly around the nativist rhetoric of former president Donald Trump and his frequent calls for the building of a border wall between the USA and Mexico. It relocates the action again, this time to the Texas-Mexico border, and follows two immigrants to Texas: Juan and Adela, played by Tenoch Huerta and Ana de la Reguera. Juan ends up working on a ranch and Adela in the meatpacking industry. After surviving the night of the Purge, the two end up caught in the "forever purge," as citizens (seemingly terminally addicted to rage and bloodshed) enact a permanent societal collapse. This is less a civil war than something closer to warlordism, as purge extremists, neo-Nazis, and fascist mobs collide with a lumpen proletariat systematically stripped of any political route to emancipation. In a sense, the film showcases the endpoint of necro-neoliberalism: an endless and inescapable violence, constantly on the hunt for a new scapegoat — in this case, Latino immigrants (the antagonists repeatedly scream at the pair to "speak English," even as the nation itself literally explodes around them). In a move seemingly borrowed from Roland Emmerich's *The Day After Tomorrow*, the Mexican border is opened to American refugees and the film stages an escape through the land of a local indigenous tribe. Having excluded any kind of revolutionary politics — even the pre-political class consciousness exemplified through organised crime in *The First Purge* — the only answer is to leave this eternal violence behind as the poor, the working class, and immigrants are either annihilated or escape.

Yet, the franchise's insistence on obfuscating the material and historical basis of violence leaves the films stuck in a kind of inescapable moralism. The New Founding Fathers may see the Purge as a tool of population control, but those who participate in it are clearly framed as having an ontological drive toward violence. Even a mainstream critic like Matt Zoller Seitz sees the film as fundamentally conservative, unable to really reckon with the hard questions it raises:

> But in the end, the film retreats into "we're all in this together, can't we get along?" posturing, landing in a centrist-to-conservative mind-space wherein we can all agree that heavily armed and openly bigoted terror groups run by Anglo-Americans are bad, and that wanting to murder rich white bigoted exploiters, while perhaps historically comprehensible, is also bad, in relation to the Ten Commandments anyway, and that once such extremists are dealt with, we can all get back to being decent to each other, which is the True American Way.[13]

Considered collectively, the two franchises both underscore the extent to which mainstream horror offers a diagnosis of the present, functioning as a cultural space in which we can see clearly the horrors of our current condition and, bleaker still, reckon with the fact that the current liberal hegemony can offer no real answers to it.

CHAPTER EIGHT

GOTHIC HISTORIOGRAPHY AND THE IDEA OF A (MONSTROUS) UTOPIA

Is it possible to think of horror and the Gothic as possessing a utopian function? For some, this question is utterly oxymoronic — in terms of affect and style, horror is predisposed toward closure, the grim realisation that one should abandon all hope; that there is, as the novel *American Psycho* opens, "No Exit." Yet, within horror there remain ineradicable traces of the past and the supernatural. If the Gothic is, as Victor Sage argues, a fantasy about history,[1] then it is also — even if only implicitly — a dream of the future. What this raises is the spectre of how the Gothic and horror put forward a vision of history that cuts against the normative enclosure of history that marks capitalist ideology. What is needed, then, is an understanding of the neglected utopian aspect within horror: namely, a recuperation of the past in which the monstrous and the supernatural become reactivated in a move toward the future. The monster is an entirely new kind of subjectivity, which has (always) struggled to emerge. Humanity, becoming itself for the very first time, would absolutely appear as monstrous — with warnings and revelations of a new kind of being. The aim here is to put the blood back into Blochian utopia; utopia isn't just an idea, a feeling, or a dream about the future, but is best understood as a politics and an existential mode of orientation toward the world. Here, then, this chapter contributes to the ongoing outworking of Bloch's philosophy of hope, finding, in the dark horrors of history, Gothic ghosts of the better world to come. To put it simply, utopia is a becoming-monstrous, a monster both within and toward the capitalist system, which both hates and fears the monsters it makes.

To begin with, it's probably worth spending a little time outlining what a utopian philosophy of history might look like, and for that, we have no better, more complete resource than the work of Ernst Bloch. For Bloch, the idea of a teleological history that could be rendered easily distinct into a past that has been left behind, a present that is lived through, and a future of smooth, easy progress is simply untenable. It is a view of history as closure — one that completely ignores history as a dynamic process. Bloch's concept of the non-synchronous nature of history in capitalism is key here. In his book *Heritage of Our Time*, he sought to offer an analysis of the rise of fascism in Weimar-era Germany. Traditionally, the left at the time is regarded as having seen fascism as essentially a corrupted ideology — a kind of political trick for which the masses had fallen. Bloch's analysis of the situation is far more interesting, and the book develops an important sociological understanding of the ways in which fascism appealed to the various strata of German society. Fascism was designed to appeal on the level of the imagination to the various different classes, and to do so successfully precisely because of what Bloch termed *Ungleichzeitigkeit* — or, in English, non-synchronicity. As he explains things:

> Not all people exist in the same Now. They do so only externally, through the fact that they can be seen today. But they are thereby not yet living at the same time with the others... Older times than the modern ones continue to have an effect in older strata; it is easy to make or dream one's way back into older ones here. Of course, a merely awkward man who for this very reason falls short of the demands of his position or little position is simply backward in himself. But what if in addition, through the continuing effect of ancient peasant origin for instance, as a type from earlier times he does not fit into a very modern concern? Various years in general beat in the one which is just being counted and prevails. Nor do they flourish in obscurity as in the past, but contradict the Now; very strangely, crookedly, from behind. The power of this untimely course has appeared, it promised precisely new life, however much it merely hauls up what is old. The masses also streamed towards it, because at least the intolerable Now seems different with Hitler, because he paints good old things for everyone. There is little more unexpected and nothing more dangerous than this power of being at once fiery and meagre, contradictory and non-contemporaneous.[2]

The model of history as being a movement from the past into the future via the medium of progress is undercut by the fundamental incompleteness of the capitalist revolution. Marxists have long written about the combined and uneven development of the capitalist mode of production, but Bloch's idea of the non-synchronic expanded this to include the degrees to which the uneven nature of capitalism inevitably carries with it cultural, social, and political impacts. This non-synchronic mode of existence is one that the socialist and communist movements of Bloch's day stubbornly ignored, being too committed to their positivist vision (which Lenin so memorably dismissed as "stupid materialism"). As mentioned above, Victor Sage calls the Gothic a kind of fantasy about history, but this is not the same thing as saying it's *untrue*. Again, Bloch provides a useful and illustrative point.

Chests are still made in Gothic form by the village carpenter for present couples with a modern date of the year, not as a fake, but as if by his father, great-grandfather and the old folk too. Despite the radio and newspapers, couples live in the village for whom Egypt is still the land where the princess dragged the boy Moses out of the river, not the land of the pyramids or the Suez Canal; it continues to be seen from the viewpoint of the Bible and the children of Israel, not from that of the Pharaoh. Konnersreuth again: the sweating of blood by the ecstatic virgin Therese Neumann there, in 1928, against the will of the much more contemporaneous bishop, denotes a different piece of Gothic in Germany. The Fichtelgebirge, the related Black Forest, and related Spessart encapsulate this kind of thing; if these mountains are no longer as gloomy and haunted as they still were in Hauff's times, raftsmen, glassblowers, spirits and robbers would be the nearest scenery surrounding such peasant Gothic even today.[3]

To think of the Gothic as a simple metaphor, aesthetic device, or some flight of fancy is to ignore the ways in which so much of the present is haunted by something that is gone but which still lingers. Time is heterogeneous: there are a plurality of possibilities within a given situation, and so the role of the Gothic Marxist is to be attentive to the patterns and currents of culture and history, to find that which still haunts. The non-synchronic is not just sociological either, but ties into Bloch's concept of subjectivity. We are internally non-synchronous, strangers to ourselves, unaware of what we are capable of in the future, while at the same time often strangers to the person that we were in the past. Bloch used the phrase "the darkness of the lived moment" to illustrate how we are so unable to reconcile ourselves to a complete and straightforward sense of self. From nations, to cultures, to class strata, and to individuals, a Gothic Marxist history is one driven by fidelity to the ghost — to the spectre that is still haunting all of the capitalist world.

The elements of the past still possess a kind of latent possibility within them, whereby their full meaning has not yet come to fruition or been fully understood. This — it should be stressed — in no way contradicts the materialism that grounds any leftist politics worth the name. Mark Fisher famously asked the younger generation why they weren't angrier at all the things they have had taken away from them — in a sense, his concept of hauntology is precisely about this sense of loss, the absence of something in the future that the culture of popular modernism seemed to promise. Yet, if the utopian project of the culture that Fisher was so drawn to seems to have vanished, its ruins and remains still haunt the contemporary imagination. Fisher's entire corpus is an attempt to wrestle with this haunting and to catalyse the latent political possibilities — from raising consciousness to the creation of new forms of social life — that capitalist realism could not completely expel. In a similar vein, the writer

Richard Gilman-Opalsky makes the argument that ghosts are the record of historical violence and exploitation — they are thus real and a natural product of the domination and violence of capitalism itself.[4] On more explicitly political grounds, Bloch's open-ended conception of history connects him with his friend and fellow philosopher Walter Benjamin.[5] Benjamin, like Bloch, was committed to the romantic critique of capitalism, highlighting its alienation, exploitation, and degradation of subjectivity. Yet this attentiveness to the non-synchronic and awareness of the potential and possibility of the past is not about getting back to some prelapsarian point, but rather is about a utopian future. For Marx, too, there is a sense that the past is never some abstract entity which is lost to us, and to think so not only cedes too much ground to the logic of capitalist inevitability, it denies revolutionary struggle a powerful resource. Think of the famous, much-quoted passage from *The Eighteenth Brumaire*:

> The tradition of all dead generations weighs like a nightmare on the brains of the living. And just as they seem to be occupied with revolutionizing themselves and things, creating something that did not exist before, precisely in such epochs of revolutionary crisis they anxiously conjure up the spirits of the past to their service, borrowing from them names, battle slogans, and costumes in order to present this new scene in world history in time-honored disguise and borrowed language. Thus Luther put on the mask of the Apostle Paul, the Revolution of 1789–1814 draped itself alternately in the guise of the Roman Republic and the Roman Empire, and the Revolution of 1848 knew nothing better to do than to parody, now 1789, now the revolutionary tradition of 1793–95.[6]

For Marx, and for Bloch, the symbols and presences of the past are not something that has to be overcome and moved beyond but something to be repurposed and allowed to work toward a new kind of future. In the context of horror, history is an active and dangerous force, a violent reemergence of an ostensibly uncivilised past into a static and inviolate present. In the Gothic, history is never over, never gone, and thus the present is never stable. The ghost always haunts, the monster always returns, the killer who disappeared thirty years ago *this very night* is always waiting behind the door when you get home. If capitalist realism seeks to impose an ideologically convenient homogeneity, then it is a stability that is deeply contingent, because the past will always re-emerge. Capitalism is haunted. Its desperate drive to impose uniformity is about exorcising the past, but it's an exorcism that will always remain, at best, incomplete. China Miéville talks about this in an old interview:

> Capitalism's early embracing of scientific thought was progressive compared to what went before, and on that basis it projects a claim that it is the triumph of systemic rationality, and that any forces which oppose it are therefore irrational or "anti-rational." But we also know that capitalism throws up, absolutely inevitably, forces which can and must oppose it. It represses just about every human impulse you can mention, which are going to resurface in various forms. Most fundamentally it throws up and represses the working class, and its emancipatory political project. It pretends class conflict is inimical to it, but it's actually integral. Monleon says, "The spectre of revolution, then, seems to be at the base of this reappearance of unreason in general, and of the fantastic in particular." So the "unreason" of fantasy is

a kind of neurotic counterpoint to capitalism's "rationality." Capitalism's "reason" produces its own monsters.[7]

To frame this in other terms, culture: 1) functions as the medium in which history can be maintained; and 2) exists to some degree within a state of semi-autonomy in relation to capitalist modes of production. As cultural production was integrated more fully into the capitalist base, this autonomy waned, but the dissolution of cultural autonomy is not to be equated with its disappearance. Culture didn't dissolve into capitalism, it exploded, and so the remnants of it exist all around us. As Jameson puts it:

> Nomic value and state power… and the very structures of the psyche itself — can be said to have become "cultural" in some original and untheorised sense… our new postmodern bodies are bereft of spatial coordinates and practically (let alone theoretically) incapable of disintantiation.[8]

It is for this reason that so much of Jameson's work has been an exercise in cognitive mapping, exploring culture to find new senses or coordinates of understanding that allow us to grasp the totality of the current historical and social conjunction and begin to think beyond it.

Where might we find those new coordinates, that sense of historicity, however fragmented, however contested? In cultural terms, in the wreckage: Benjamin has his ragpicker, and Mieville talks about salvage theory[9] as a mode of intellectual production, both of which are powerful and useful theoretical images of thought. If capitalism has become more cultural, culture has also become more capitalist — films are reverse-engineered to start franchises, artificially generating their own fandoms before they have even been released, but this doesn't exhaust the potential of popular culture or negate the importance of continuing to search for what Benjamin would call the profane illuminations of our current condition. Horror, in particular, has always been seen as critically disreputable by the mainstream for the majority of its history, and that alone should attract attention. This is the importance of Gothic Marxism as both a hermeneutics and a philosophy of history. Bloch's own work was fascinated with popular culture, with everything from the folk stories and fairy tales of the rural poor to the adventure stories of writers like Karl May, to the detective stories of Arthur Conan Doyle and Edgar Allan Poe. For Bloch, popular culture was a storehouse of utopian thought and possibility, and so, in horror, we find the possibility of a reawakened past — dangerous, fragmented, but never entirely eliminated. Thomas Ligotti's short stories are an excellent example of how this history (which in capitalist modernity is almost relentlessly connected to the irrational) is both terrifying and yet also revolutionary. One only need see something like the decay of the buildings in *My Work Is Not Yet Done*,[10] or the town of Mirocaw in "The Last Feast of Harlequin," where protagonists come face-to-face with the terrifying otherness of the long-thought-lost irrational past, which drives them ultimately to madness. While the textual politics of the Gothic and horror are often ambiguous at best and outright reactionary at worst, this does not necessarily negate the overall idea of a Gothic Marxist hermeneutics. Jameson, in one of the earliest English-language engagements with Bloch's work, points out that his hermeneutics finds its richness in

the very variety of its objects themselves while its initial conceptual content remains relatively simple, relatively unchanging: thus little by little wherever we look everything in the world becomes a version of some primal figure, a manifestation of that primordial movement towards the future and toward ultimate identity with a transfigured world which is Utopia, and in whose vital presence, behind whatever distortions, beneath whatever layers of repression, may always be detected, no matter how faintly, by the instruments and apparatuses of hope itself.[11]

A good example of this in the context of contemporary horror would be something like Liam Gavin's 2016 film *A Dark Song*. It follows a grief-stricken woman, Sophia (Catherine Walker), who hires a taciturn medium, Joseph Solomon (Steve Oram). Sophia wants to conduct the Abramelin ritual to summon her guardian angel in order to bring her dead son back to life. As a character, she is both haunting and haunted; living constantly in the moment of her own child's death, she is, in effect, trapped in her own past. As the ritual drags on, becoming more intensive, and the relationship between Joseph and Sophia breaks down into mental and sexual coercion, it is revealed that what she wants is not the restoration of her son but rather to take revenge on the person who kidnapped and murdered the child. Yet this act of magical revenge is twisted as Joseph dies and demons begin to appear in the house to torture her. Yet, right at the close, with Sophia lost in the dark, bloodied, and in pain, the guardian angel appears. A genuinely fantastic piece of cinematic magic, its presence is almost too much to look at — Sophia asks for the power to forgive, and there the film ends. She walks from the house, into the new. In her case, she's been freed to live without the perhaps justifiable desire to restage new kinds of violence in the world — all thanks to an almost Messianic utopian intervention. This represents the way in which horror has a utopian function, both reopening history on the macro-level while at the same time fundamentally reshaping human subjectivity.

In an era when so much popular culture simply restages the issues of the day or lapses into easy, genre-based optimism, horror stubbornly refuses to either opt out of the possibility of change or to buy hope on the cheap. Jameson points out that for Bloch there are two great enemies of hope: the first is memory, and the second, fear.[12] Both are concerned with a retreat from possibility and a return to what *was* — again, in *A Dark Song* this tension gets a creative outworking and resolution. The film shows Sophia's fear, her memories of loss, and everything that keeps her trapped within the past. Due to an accident, Solomon, the occultist, is injured, and the wound becomes infected; and as he lays dying, he tells Sophia that this means the ritual is working and she will get the revenge that she wants. And yet, when confronted with the moment of choice between memory and fear on the one side, and the possibility of hope on the other, Sophia asks for nothing aside from the possibility of a new future.

Thus a Gothic Marxist philosophy of history recuperates the flotsam and jetsam of capitalist realism, and finds within this low-brow, blood-stained form of culture a utopian possibility. However, this raises the necessary requirement of outlining in more detail what kind of utopia this might be. Utopian philosophy can generally be said to fall into two camps: the programmatic, on the one hand, and on the other, a tendency more concerned with the spirit of utopianism.[13] In the wake of the twentieth century, programmes for utopia are in short supply, and perhaps rightly so. But if Gothic Marxism can articulate a utopianism, it is a utopia for the monstrous and the monstered.

Again, the monster is both a warning and a revelation, an ambiguous double sign that repulses and attracts at the same time — think of the body of the creature in *Frankenstein*, racialised, brutalised, and ignored, which became a symbol of the emergent political power of a working class that was able to speak back (in revolutionary terms) against its oppressors. For a modern example, think of the zombie as outlined in the filmography of George A. Romero. In Romero's films, the zombie becomes the face of alienated mid-twentieth-century subjectivity, condemned to wander endlessly through shopping malls. Yet, throughout Romero's films, it is slowly revealed that the hordes of creatures are conscious, able to feel pain, to organise, and to express a new kind of subjectivity. The monster is a becoming-subject, a new thing that finds expression in the darkest places of human culture. This is in contrast to that other tradition of monstrous language, capitalism itself. These Gothic metaphors should not be discarded, even as we seek to recuperate the figure of the monster from the icy grip of ideologues who seek to instrumentalise it. The language of the Gothic and horror with which capitalism can be accurately described aims precisely to denaturalise the systems which produce the rationalised sadism of contemporary capitalism. We are all subjected to this, and so to describe capitalism in these terms is not to make it into something new but to pry away the mask of ideology and reveal the horror beneath. We must, in order to forge a future, become *monsters against the monstrosity of capitalism.*

The implication here is that this utopianism, the futurity of Gothic Marxism, is not some benign universalism — how could it be, when (as China Miéville points out) we live in a utopia; it just isn't ours.[14] Our current utopia belongs to the capitalist class that would choke the earth to death and target the poor in their Malthusian apocalypticism. There is a utopia now, but the utopia of the monster necessarily requires the destruction of the current utopia of the capitalist. We must, in other words, "learn to hope with teeth."[15] If there is a utopia to come, it will be for those who right now are monstered. The monster contains a utopian excess that cuts against the grain of the so-called real world. The Gothic Marxist utopia is that of a communised community of the monstered monsters — or to put this more plainly: it is a communist utopia. But again, lest we get dragged into arguments about program, party, or concrete policy, it is worth pointing out that, as Adam Jones puts it,

> it is pointless to talk of how the world will be "under" communism — communism is the underworld, the site where life exceeds itself and points to something more, hidden under the skin of the hegemonic social body. Within the communist underworld there will be monsters, but none monstered. There will be contradiction, the monster will continue to speak, but the meaning of the particularity, the anarchic abnormal, will be liberated from its constraints which relegated the activity of its living contradiction to contradicting the very monstering universality which monstered it. The monsters will speak to each other and make without monstering, for we are all monstrous in varying degrees, for we are all particular. This is even true of hegemonic, capitalist universality, which frantically denies this of itself and denies it of us in monstering the demonstrations of its own monstrosity.[16]

The final point here is perhaps the most important — we are all monsters, or, at least, can all easily be made into them. Monsters' continuing appeal is not to be found in their distance from us but rather in its complete opposite: the vampire is us, or at least comprises the desire within us to treat others as objects for our own consumption. We look at the zombie mass, wandering through the shattered remnant of a world of consumerist and extractive capitalism, and we see ourselves. There are important commonalities here with Evan Calder Williams's notion of capitalist apocalypse. Williams talks of the ways in which capitalism produces the "undifferentiated," or "those things which cannot be included in the realm of the openly visible without rupturing the very oppositions which make the whole enterprise move forward".[17] For Williams — and this is also true of a monstrous Utopia — the point of the capitalist apocalypse is not that the end of things might result in a better, more inclusive, and kinder new thing coming into being; if anything, it's quite the opposite: the task is "the ceaseless struggle to dismantle and repurpose… to articulate militant reason out the obscene persistence of that which refuses to die."[18]

The monster refuses to die. And whenever it does die, it will always return — it is in this sense of historical inevitability that we find the hope of horror, hard won and blood soaked. The monster is the avatar of the new appearing into the tortured stasis of capitalist realism. Capitalism creates its monsters and hates them — the vampire bride must always be staked through the heart, and the zombie must be tied to a table to endure a horrific vivisection in the name of capitalist rationality. The potential transformation — the new that the monster heralds — is both sublime and terrifying, presupposing that we, too, can be changed into something that we may not recognise. This is where the Blochian non-synchronous meets our own individual darkness of the lived moment. In the monster, we see not only something that can return us to history, reclaiming the incomplete past, but a force which requires us to acknowledge our shared commonality with it. In other words, we're all monsters now: if there is a Gothic Marxism, it is one that demands solidarity with the monster(ed) and with the incomplete historical revolution that it represents.

CONCLUSION

WE'RE ALL MONSTERS NOW

Why wilt thou Examine every little fibre of my soul
Spreading them out before the Sun like Stalks of flax to dry
The infant joy is beautiful but its anatomy
Horrible Ghast & Deadly nought shalt thou find in it
But Death Despair & Everlasting brooding Melancholy
Thou wilt go mad with horror if thou dost Examine thus
Every moment of my secret hours.

William Blake, *The Four Zoas*

I'm not going to write about the future, again. I'm not going to write about no-future, either. I'll write about the process of becoming other.

Franco Berardi

Facing the various monstrosities of the present, what will it take to rescue and reclaim a future? Is this not the primary question of a present that forces us to reckon with our contingency and ultimately our own disposability? How do we deal with the horrifying reality of the present as the necropolitical violence of capitalism scythes outward ever wider? If there is to be any ground for hope in the cultural imagination, it has to come from forms of culture that are up to the task of hoping with teeth, of taking on, unflinchingly, the stakes involved and refusing both a collapse into nihilistic despair or an all-too-easy platitudinous optimism of some techno-future that will fix all the problems. In contemporary horror, we find space that allows for a multiplicity of engagements with our own monstrous condition — in Alison Rumfitt's novel *Tell Me I'm Worthless*, we see the ways in which monstrosity is not a natural category but one driven by the violence of a capitalist system which depends upon the creation and expulsion of the "monstrous." Both within and against capitalism, the monstrous is produced by the same system it will eventually overcome. Here, Gothic Marxism forms the dark shadow or dialectical inverse of the psychedelia of Mark Fisher's acid communism, with both of these approaches serving as powerful ways of understanding our potential capacity for transforming ourselves and the world around us.

The modern monster is not natural. While the monsters of antiquity were certainly presented as a part of the natural world, contemporary monsters are produced; or to put it another way, monsters are, like many other metaphors, manmade.[1] From the moment of their creation, what makes monsters so simultaneously attractive and terrifying is not their strangeness but how similar they are to us. Think back again to Frankenstein's creature: what inspires fear in Victor is not simply the fact that the creature is stitched together from the bodies of the poor and the dead he's vivisected (a fact that we seem to gloss over in talking about *Frankenstein*), but that the body he brings to life can *speak*, and even worse, can speak in the same Enlightenment and rationalist terms of the educated Victor. "Hear me, Frankenstein," demands the creature, and the violent refusal of Victor to grant any audience or recognition to what he has brought into being is instrumental in the enforcement of the category of the monster. This isn't just a cultural or literary device either — the violence of imperialism and colonialism rests upon the notion of the other being something non-human. The slavery that built the wealth of America and the British empire as well as the violence of apartheid were all perpetuated and sustained by the retributive fear of a phantasmatic monstrous violence.

To put this another way, the creation of the monster is a political act; "monster" is a category that has to be both produced and enforced, but it's also a category that remains unstable and, in some ways — as Paul Preciado points out — still to be determined. Victor Frankenstein thought of his creation as a vile monster, but the creature reads Milton before coming face-to-face with his creator and asking for recognition. Try as he might, Victor cannot deal with the fact that the creature is more than he expects. To put this in slightly more philosophical terms, there is a *surplus of meaning* within the monster, both a warning and a revelation of the new breaking into the present. As a result, it's really not a surprise that monsters have been adopted by those who find themselves being monstered themselves. The Babadook (from Jennifer Kent's 2014 film of the same name) as a gay icon might be a meme online,[2] but it also expresses something of the ways in which heteronormative capitalist hegemony has seen queerness as a monstrous threat to the norm, especially to discourses of family and childhood innocence. The flip side of this is the utopian potentiality of monstrosity, of that which lies *beyond the horizon of the Now.* Monsters point to something, a new way of being, that lies somewhere out there on the horizon of our shared social life. This is something that the last half-century of history underscores with its record of cultural panic about non-heterosexuality, the disciplinary pathologisation of homosexuality, of queer relationships, and of queer sex. To be different is to leave oneself open to being made monstrous, made into something that provokes fear and panic in a particular cultural moment and set of political discourses. Accordingly, the last decade or so has seen a new category of monstrosity summoned: that of trans people.

The British media in particular, after decades excelling at demonising and monstering gay and lesbian people in the most revolting ways, have turned with sweaty eagerness to spreading the most virulent anti-trans rhetoric, continuing the very essence of UK journalism. All of this has accelerated with a spate of anti-trans legislation across much of the USA and the ever-escalating and dehumanising rhetoric directed against trans people that has become a near-permanent fixture in UK politics. It should be emphasised that many of these issues intersect with the wider misogynistic and homophobic politics of the current moment — none of this is *new*; rather, it is an intensification and acceleration of already-existing tendencies within the present. Thus, we haven't got new monsters *per se*, but rather monstrosity as a retooled category for the cultural politics of the present moment. Accordingly, much of the rhetoric and language around these political questions consistently frames trans people as a threat, as predators, monsters at the door of the normative, supposedly heterosexual, white family unit. The cry against the monster is the hysterical imperative: "Won't someone think of the children." Lock them away, keep them out of school, don't let them go online, don't let them talk to one another — there are monsters out there.

How must it feel for those forced to reckon with the horror of a world that sees them only as monsters? What ways out of and through these violent systems might there be? Is it possible to think about this process, this enforced category of being made monstrous, as a ground for a kind of utopian thinking? This might sound slightly antithetical, but it is precisely the surplus of meaning within the category of the monster that is at stake in this conjunction. If there is a way out, toward the utopian ideal that Ernst Bloch called *Heimat*, wherein all people can, as he put it, "walk upright for the first time," then it will be found *first* by those who have been monstered.

From a more philosophical point of view, this is simply because the figure of the monster is almost always out of time (something they share with communists!) — they are harbingers of the future in the past and present. It's worth pointing out that the monstering of trans people never seems to occur in isolation and is bound up with wider political concerns. As mentioned back in chapter five, Judith Butler, among others, has made explicit the links between attacks on so-called gender ideology and a deeper, more widespread reactionary turn in politics. Transphobia, then, is a symptom of a wider fascist backlash. We have to pay attention to it, because the category of monster is *mobile*: where one monster is found, this new reactionary-fascist politics will quickly find others.

In *Tell Me I'm Worthless*, the type of monstrosity in question seems initially like a haunting — "SORRY FOR LETTING YOU HAUNT THIS BOOK", the reader is told, but this is nothing but a lesson in culpability. The whole point of the novel is that fascism is a kind of *presence*, something that accretes over time, a miasma emerging from the rot that is right under your feet. The issue isn't so much the fascism that we're all used to, with its flags and marching (though that is absolutely a part of it); rather, it's the fascism that is under your own skin, behind your own eyes, that's made its way inside your own head already.

The novel follows Alice, Ila and Hannah, three friends who spend a night in a haunted house. Something immensely traumatic happens, the exact details of which are deliberately kept occluded throughout the majority of the book. Some years after the fact, Alice is deeply traumatised, trapped in a depressive anhedonia supported by drugs, drinking too much, and survival sex work found through the web. She is completely estranged from Ila, who has fully embraced the fascist politics of British so-called gender-critical feminism (which is, of course, not critical about gender and shouldn't be considered feminist in any real sense of the term). Hannah is missing, and the two decide to go to the house to confront what happened. It is a novel deeply rooted in the political questions of contemporary Britain, and the question of politics is never abstract or impersonal but lived out in the body, especially in the bodies of those that contemporary culture sees as its monsters (the novel makes explicit that the violence of transphobia is directly connected not just to misogynistic violence against all women but to xenophobic hatred of outsiders generally). Perfidious Albion is a vast decaying mansion, built and maintained through violence that is omnipresent. The house is the concretisation of the bloody heart of Britain, the reification of the libidinal politics that eats tabloid headlines, gorging itself on them till sick. The haunted house/fascism connection is a useful tool for contemporary horror, and pops up in works like Silvia Moreno-Garcia's excellent fungal-fascist horror *Mexican Gothic*. But Rumfitt makes central the notion of desire that involves *you* as a reader, external to the text. You don't get to stand outside this novel and watch what unfolds, because you live here already — or to put this another way, the category of the monster is one that can all too easily be turned back upon you. Look what you've done, and what's worse, look at *how much you enjoy doing it*. There's a short chapter toward the end of the novel entitled "House" that addresses the reader:

> You, too, are implicated in its presence. Don't forget that. You, me. Those you love… Your housemate and your lover and your queen. Your MP and your favorite author… so on and so on forever until I can't speak anymore, and my words become one long eternal howl.[3]

The questions of both space and history are inescapable here — the novel points out that this is what distinguishes a haunted-house story from a ghost story: haunted houses are about architecture and time. If the internet is a haunted ruin, the novel makes the same allegorical point about contemporary British society. We live in an all-encompassing web of micro-fascisms, and the novel details what this feels like to live through. This is horror as a kind of anti-fascism, as a way of trying to answer a question of political philosophy that goes back to Spinoza: Why do people desire their own repression? The novel's answer is, in part at least: because there's something about it which is libidinally thrilling, but also because the pain it offers is familiar. There's a horrific moment toward the end of the novel when the beautiful, blonde-haired Hannah is twisted into a swastika. She spews the most vile hate at her friends as the house makes its way into her consciousness, and her reward is to be transformed into a symbolic representation of fascist ideology. Her bones crack and her body is mangled almost beyond recognition, and in her last moments of lucidity, the reader hears her say to the house "you told me I'd be safe." Isn't it better, the house asks, to feel that familiar pain of what we all already know than face the nightmare possibility of a world of freedom?

Fascism gets into your head. This system that produces monsters is both a vast historical structure and deeply and personally bound up with the social field. But, of course, much as the fascist might want otherwise, desire is not *natural*. We have to be taught to desire, we have to learn these libidinal investments, and as the novel shows, we are all remarkably keen students. It's no wonder, then, that the monster is hated. The right-wing politics of Britain hates its monsters not because of their gross excesses (the right's hysterical invocations of degeneracy are a remarkable and telling self-indictment), but precisely because the monster can speak, can self-make and self-fashion — can *love* — in ways which reveal the rot, the empty husk that squats at the core of right-wing political ontology. If there is a utopia here, or even the possibility of one, it rests upon precisely that love. Toward the end of the novel, there's a long chapter which isn't (as all the previous chapters are) titled after characters from the text; instead it's titled "You." It closes with these lines:

> They embrace, covered in each other's insides. *I love you, says* Ila. *I love you, says* Alice. And the world comes crashing down around them. Maybe they'll be okay. Do you think they'll be okay, in the end? I think they will be. I have to think they will be.[4]

The novel isn't just a critique of the insidious fascism that undergirds the political imagination of the present; it's also about the fundamentally double-edged sword of desire. It's useful for fascist politics, but desire is never predetermined, and so to think that way is to recognise the extent to which things *can be different.* The novel's epilogue, which takes place at a Pride march (full of resonances with John Berger's famous point about the nature of protest: that it is fundamentally a rehearsal for revolution), is shattered by violence again, but it closes with people holding one another, even at the very end. Love is thus never simply a kind of subjective romanticism; it possesses a universality embodied in those who have been cast out and made into monsters. The positive moments toward the novel's climax are all about the ways in which we can become something and someone else. There's a small moment right at the end of the novel when a character looks back at the person they once were. They experience that glorious feeling of disidentification in which a person can look back at oneself and see pain and suffering without re-experiencing it anew. Personal identity becomes something more fluid, and those negative experiences from the past become something that all but happened to someone else, someone from another time. There's a chance, right? Perhaps we all might be so lucky. As Ernst Bloch puts it in a striking passage from his book *The Principle of Hope*, these moments, these snapshots of something new coming into being, "are not merely those things that have not appeared, but those that are not decided, they dawn in mere real possibility, and contain the danger of possible disaster, but also the hope of possible, still not thwarted happiness."[5] Do you think they'll be okay in the end? I think they will be. Haunted houses can't always be exorcised, capitalist history cannot so easily be wiped away, but as the end of *Tell Me I'm Worthless* shows, haunted houses can be burnt down, and in their ashes there might be a new kind of world come into being even if only for a single moment.

It's the question of the new world that concerns Gretchen Felker-Martin's *Manhunt*. A grindhouse, pulp twist on the common idea of the gendercide novel (think *Y: The Last Man*, *Afterland*, or *The Men*), it takes seriously the question of what it might mean to survive when the world has to be remade, while at the same time trying to unpick the gender-essentialist logic and often explicit transphobia that undergirds so much of the form. In the wake of the estrophaga "t. rex" virus, which turns anyone with high-enough testosterone in their system into a cannibalistic rapist covered in pus-oozing sores, the novel takes seriously the same questions of desire and politics that *Tell Me I'm Worthless* does, but it escalates the fundamentally embodied nature of those questions. The novel follows two trans women, Fran and Beth, as they try to survive by harvesting the testicles of feral men to keep their hormone levels in check. Again, as with so many of the texts discussed here, the fundamental politics at stake are embodied — in this case, on the endocrinological level. After all, when the structures and institutions that do so much to obfuscate and elide the violence of the present are no longer there (because… well, at the end of the world, close to nothing is), this political embodiment shouldn't be a surprise. If the gendercide novel rests upon an unspoken (or occasionally very proudly spoken) exclusion of gender-non-conforming bodies, trans men and women, and the intersex, *Manhunt* functions as an attempt to expose the ways in which essential notions of gender see these bodies as fundamentally disposable. Or, as Felker-Martin put it in an interview, the conceit of the virus was "about implementing this idea that would make it very plain who is operating in a state of vulnerability in our world and who might have some social protection."[6] There is no need to "say the quiet part loud" in the world of *Manhunt* anymore. The novel's violence and graphic body horror underscore the ways in which desire is not abstract but embodied, literally enfleshed in visceral ways. Toward the beginning of the novel, there's a moment when Beth finds herself thinking of these monsters that had once been men:

> Beth wondered if they were lonely, those things that had been men. If they missed their wives, their mothers, their daughters and girlfriends and dominatrixes. Or maybe they were happy now, free to rape and kill and eat whomever, free to shit and piss and jerk off in the street. Maybe this world was the one they'd always wanted.[7]

There are echoes here of Paul Preciado's point, in his work *Can the Monster Speak?*, about the fundamentally fabricated nature of normative, "natural" masculinity:

> The masculinity you adopt and endorse is no less fabricated than mine. You would need only to review your history of normalization and submission to the dominant social and political codes of gender and sexuality in order to feel the spinning wheel of fabrication whirl inside you once more and with it the desire to break free of the repetition, to disidentify.[8]

Beth's thought is so melancholy because it contains within it the implicit possibility that things could have been different, that one could look at the monstrosity before you and recognise that — *despite everything* — it didn't have to end this way. So much of contemporary misogyny blames women for the violence of men — naturalising it with the excuse that this is just how men are, after all. The novel's brilliance is in taking this heinous logic to breaking point, underscoring the hollowness of these gender-essentialist arguments.

For all of the violence and pain at the end of the world, there is another Blochian point at work here: namely that genesis lies at the end of things and not the beginning. Endings are, by their very nature, the precondition of something new coming into being. The novel spends a great deal of time examining the various kinds of new formations that come into being at the end of the world. There is the "bunker brat" Sophie Widdel, some sort of tech heiress who uses their vast wealth and institutional power to recreate a world eerily similar to the one which has ended. For Fran, who passes, Sophie and the bunker represent a chance for an assimilationist existence — one of comfort and protection. Beth, on the other hand, does not pass, and thus needs and deserves a different form of solidarity and social belonging — and the novel manages to give both characters compelling internal monologues.

The novel's treatment of both characters underscores the extent to which the desire to belong has a kind of orthogonal solidarity with the self-loathing inflicted when belonging is not possible under current conditions. After all, it's only when we recognise our own fundamental alienation from the present state of things that we can start to engage with the project of building a better world. For Beth, the bunker represents a new kind of imprisoning — it's a place in which her desires are still seen as a threat. In fact, this is exactly what happens: when Beth makes the mistake of reciprocating the desire of another, she is punished, sent to work as a "daddy" to service the sexual needs of the bunker's inhabitants. Later, she's commodified again, being made part of a "labour exchange" when she is forced out of the bunker and handed over to the other form of societal organisation that has arisen in the ashes of the old world — a fascist paramilitary TERF (trans-exclusionary radical feminist) militia.

The Maryland Womyn's Legion represents both the persistence of transphobia and the ways in which violence toward that which is labelled monstrous is framed in terms of a kind of safety. The legion begins murdering trans women as a security measure — the logic goes that, without the right hormones, they will reveal themselves to be the men that they always already were. The aim of the legion is a militarised, female utopia — one that relies on strict and immutable ideas of gender and has no use for the edge case or the messy reality and mutability of subjectivity. The fear of the other is a beginning point for necropolitical violence, for the domination and eradication of the other is always the acceptable price of safety. Yet, even within the TERF army, there are aspects of a desire that cuts against the fascist libidinal economy; the chaser Ramona is presented as essentially caught between her own self-hatred and self-disgust and the vindication that her outward adherence to the violent annihilationist politics of the legion supplies her with.

What is striking about *Manhunt* is that the determinedly low-brow pulp aesthetic is married to a keen political awareness. The dangers of the bunker brat and the TERF army are relatively clear, but the novel is also unsparing in its criticism of milquetoast and apolitical queer culture. In perhaps one of the funniest passages in the entire book, Beth thinks back to her time with the Flying Saucer Collective (a communal, queer-friendly home that threw her out as soon as the news about the virus broke). Their apparent radical acceptance — signified by asymmetrical haircuts and pride pins — can't disguise the fact that they see Beth as "the man you've always been, and you'll never be anything else."[9] With gallows humour, Beth thinks that "it was actually good that the world had ended, because no-one would make her play Settlers of Catan."[10]

The depoliticised aesthetics of apparently kind inclusion collapse into a passive adherence to authority. That said, as a vision of the future, there is one final model through which to think about horror's potential utopian function. Toward the end of the novel, with the bunker (and its brat) destroyed, and the TERF army becoming increasingly dangerous, the remaining survivors come across Fort Dyke — an old coastal battery renovated and occupied by a group that refused both the assimilationist life of the bunker and the violent oppression of the TERF army. The group take in the survivors, and the place is fortified; there, Beth finds for the first time a sense of sisterhood, and the group turn out to be explicitly anti-fascist in a way that the long-gone Flying Saucer Collective could never hope to be. They decide to take the fight to the enemy — the fight is bloody and hard, and not everyone survives, but there is a *kind* of victory. As Felker-Martin put it in an interview:

> I believe really firmly that trans people and queer people can build the world that they want together. And that even though it's miserable and it's endless work and it's really shoveling shit against the tide in so many different situations, it can be done. And the work is worth doing on its own merits, because what is the point of eking out an existence if nobody loves you... Politics is who you love and who you're willing to kill. That's really it. And I think that if you don't come to politics willing to fight for what you believe, willing to throw away the idea that consensus and assimilation are necessary end goals, what are you doing?[11]

To put it simply, utopia must be fought for. Horror is useful as a form in that it shows that the desire for utopia is fraught, riven with violence, and that a naive passive liberalism that depends upon the institutions of the capitalist present is entirely and completely insufficient. As discussed, the novel posits several different models of commonality and being together: from the beautiful and joyous eroticism of its fucking, on the one hand, to the vicious subordination and self-annihilation of its TERF-fascist cults caught in the grip of both unspoken desire and drives toward domination on the other. The body is a site of great pain and often of violence and trauma, but also of a kind of limitless possibility that can be remade and, through that process, participate in the remaking of the world around it. Without spoiling too much more of the novel, there is a kind of hope at the end for those who survive, but (as Bloch's philosophy so exhaustively details) utopia is not a place but a process, and thus that process is made by those who are made by the process itself. The new — that drive toward utopia that is catalysed by the incomplete ghosts of the past — does not require some kind of perfectible subject; rather, it requires the courage to look into the unknown, to accept the monstrous transformations of becoming new.

We live in an age of horror — as a polyphonic, multivalent mode of culture and as a structuring metaphor that can function as both diagnosis and as utopian aspiration. The Gothic and horror show that change is always possible; try as it might to prove otherwise, capitalism is haunted by something: what the theorist Mark Fisher called (borrowing a line from Herbert Marcuse) the "specter of a world that would be free." Bloch wrote that only Marxism was both detective and liberator — only in an expansive view of human culture can a truly liberatory cultural politics be constructed, even from the very darkest of places. If there is a utopian future to be made, it is one that includes all that haunts the capitalist imagination, every scrap of culture that incessantly whispers to us that the world does not have to be this way. It is a utopian notion to see the Gothic and horror not as a kind of closure of the possible but as an expansion of what could be; it is a gamble to believe that even in the darkest products of culture, in the midst of violence, horror and despair, there is the unmistakable trace of hope, glittering under the blood. But when the stakes are so high, when the current situation is so bleak, all resources are needed in order to find ways out and through the haunted ruins of a necrotic neoliberalism that both chokes off the imagination and limits the horizons of political possibility. To pay attention to the ghost, to the monster, the strange, and the supernatural is to find new methods of comprehending not only our past but the possibility of the future, thus undertaking the vital work of bolstering the utopian imagination. China Miéville puts the problem in useful terms: "We know that even many who love us are bewildered by our unrealism… our utopian foolishness, in striving for what we strive for: but can you understand how unrealistic their beliefs are to us?"[12] A Gothic Marxism is one that is alive to the possibilities of what seems to be unrealistic, finding in the haunting persistence of ghosts and monsters the dark traces of what Ursula Le Guin called the realism of a larger reality. Gothic Marxism rejects both the positivist dogma of uncritical thought and the instrumentalist logic of capitalist realism, embracing the monstrous potential of a future that is still to be made.

THE END

Notes

INTRODUCTION: A SPECTRE IS HAUNTING US ALL

1   Nancy Fraser, *Cannibal Capitalism: How Our System Is Devouring Democracy, Care, and the Planet — and What We Can Do About It* (London: Verso Books 2022).

2   All quotes from Marx's work are taken from the widely available archive hosted at Marxists.org. This quote is from *Capital* Volume One, Chapter One: https://www.marxists.org/archive/marx/works/1867-c1/ch01.htm

3   In response to this critique, the new translation of Ludovico Silva's *Marx's Literary Style* could hardly be more timely — considering Marx's metaphors as scientific categories constitutes a kind of epistemological and hermeneutic violence that reduces his work to a set of schema rather than the open-ended and ongoing critique they actually are. See: Ludovico Silva, *Marx's Literary Style* (London: Verso Books, 2023).

4   Mark Steven, *Splatter Capital: The Political Economy of Gore Films* (London: Repeater Books 2016).

5   See: http://v21collective.org/manifesto-of-the-v21-collective-ten-theses/

6   Quoted in: Margaret Cohen, *Profane Illuminations: Walter Benjamin and the Paris of Surrealist Revolution* (Berkley: University of California Press 1995) p. 15.

7   Ernst Fischer, *The Necessity of Art*, 2nd edition (London: Verso Books 2010).

8   See: Walter Benjamin, "Conversations with Brecht," *New Left Review*, (Jan/Feb 1973), available online at: https://newleftreview.org/issues/i77/articles/walter-benjamin-conversations-with-brecht

9   Walter Benjamin, "On The Concept of History" trans. Dennis Redmond. Avaliable online here: https://www.marxists.org/reference/archive/benjamin/1940/history.htm

10   Stanley Mitchell, "Introduction to Benjamin and Brecht," *New Left Review*, I/77 (Jan/Feb 1973) p. 43.

11   Walter Benjamin, *The Arcades Project*, trans. Howard Eiland and Kevin McLaughlin (Harvard: Harvard University Press 1999) p. 462.

12   Anthony Auerbach, "Imagine No Metaphors: The Dialectical Image of Walter Benjamin," *Image and Narrative*, 18, (September 2007), available online at: https://www.imageandnarrative.be/inarchive/thinking_pictures/auerbach.htm

13   Enzo Traverso, *Revolution: An Intellectual Biography* (London: Verso Books 2021).

14   Fredric Jameson, "Introduction/prospectus: To reconsider the relationship of marxism to utopian thought," *The Minnesota Review*, NS6 (1976) pp. 53–58.

15   Mark Storey and Steven Shapiro, "American Horror, Genre and History," in *The Cambridge Companion to American Horror* (Cambridge: Cambridge University Press 2022) pp. 1–12.

16   Listen to *Horror Vanguard* wherever you find your podcasts. And for a book-length articulation of the argument that horror wants to do things to your body, see: Xavier Aldana Reyes, *Horror Film and Affect: Towards a Corporeal Model of Viewership* (London: Routledge 2016).

17   See Clarke's interview at: https://www.newyorker.com/magazine/2020/09/14/susanna-clarkes-fantasy-world-of-interiors

CHAPTER ONE: THE DARK WAY OF BEING RED

1   All of this is best summarised in the collection *Aesthetics and Politics* (London: Verso Books 1997), which not only collects the various exchanges between the participants but also adds a deeply helpful essay from Fredric Jameson, contextualising and clarifying the stakes of the argument.

2   Ernst Bloch, *The Principle of Hope vol 1*, trans Neville Plaice, Stephen Plaice and Paul Knight. (Harvard: MIT Press 1995) p. 208.

3   Ibid., p. 209.

4   Ibid.

5   See Mark Steven's book *Splatter Capital* for a tour-de-force exploration of this in the context of the horror cinema of the twentieth century.

6   See http://v21collective.org/manifesto-of-the-v21-collective-ten-theses/

7   All of this is extensively catalogued in György Lukacs's sadly little-read book *The Destruction of Reason* (London: Verso Books 2021) — a new edition with an extremely useful introduction from Alberto Toscano.

8   Michael Löwy and Robert Sayre, "Figures of Romantic Anti-Capitalism," *New German Critique*, 32 (1984) p. 48.

9   Ibid., p. 49.

10 For explorations of precisely this issue, see Angela Wright, *Britain, France and the Gothic, 1764–1820: The Import of Terror* (Cambridge: Cambridge University Press 2013), and Diane Long Hoevler, *The Gothic Ideology, Religious Hysteria and anti-Catholicism in British Popular Fiction, 1780–1880* (Cardiff: University of Wales Press 2014).

11 There are plenty of examples of this, but for a good overview of the link between imagination and politics, see China Miéville who talks about the prophetic mode of address utilised by the

Communist Manifesto. See China Miéville, *A Spectre Haunting: On The Communist Manifesto,* (London: Head of Zeus 2021).

12   Ernst Bloch, *The Principle of Hope Vol 1* trans. Stephen Plaice, Neville Plaice and Paul Knight (Harvard: MIT Press 1995) p. xxxii

13   Jurgen Habermas, "Ernst Bloch: A Marxist Romantic," *Salmagundi* (1969, autumn-winter), p 315.

14   Famously discussed by Neitzsche in *Ecce Homo*, available online at: https://www.gutenberg.org/files/52190/52190-h/52190-h.htm

15   Jurgen Habermas, "Ernst Bloch: A Marxist Romantic," *Salmagundi (*1969, autumn-winter), p 316.

16   For an essential read on the relevance of Nietzsche to leftist thinking, see the excellent book by Jonas Čeika, *How To Philosophise With a Hammer and Sickle: Nietzsche and Marx for the 21st Century* (London: Repeater Books 2021).

17   Michael Löwy, *Morning Star: Surrealism, Marxism, Anarchism, Situationism, Utopia,* (Austin: University of Texas Press 2009), p. 22.

18   Ibid.

19   See Walter Benjamin, "Surrealism, the last Snapshot of the European Intelligentsia." In *One Way Street and Other Writings,* trans. Edmund Jephcott, and Kingsley Shorter, (London: New Left Books 1979) pp. 225–240, p. 239.

20   Margaret Cohen, *Profane Illumination: Walter Benjamin and the Paris of Surrealist Revolution* (Berkeley: University of California Press 1995), pp. 1–2.

CHAPTER TWO: LIFE AND DEATH IN CAPITALIST MODERNITY

1   Xu Lizhi, "I Fell Asleep, Just Standing Like That," available online at: https://www.poetryfoundation.org/harriet-books/2014/11/xu-lizhi-1990-2014-poet-and-foxconn-worker-

2   See the essay "Good for Nothing", published in The Occupied
    Times (2014). Available here: https://theoccupiedtimes.
    org/?p=12841

3   Available online at: https://www.marxists.org/archive/marx/
    works/1848/communist-manifesto/ch01.htm#007

4   Available online at: https://www.marxists.org/archive/
    marx/works/1848/communist-manifesto/ch02.htm. For a
    contemporary defense and rearticulation of the communist idea
    of family abolition, see the extremely important work by Sophie
    Lewis, *Abolish the Family: A Manifesto for Care and Liberation* (London:
    Verso Books 2022).

5   I borrow the term micro-work from Phil Jones, *Work without The
    Worker: Labour in The Age of Platform Capitalism* (London: Verso
    Books 2021).

6   Baek Min, for *Tropics of Meta*, reads the relationship in Lacanian
    terms and sees the sex scene between Park Dong-ik and his wife,
    Choi Yeon-gyo, in which they imagine the sexual relationships
    between their employees, as a symbolic sexual assault on the
    Kim patriarch: https://tropicsofmeta.com/2020/02/23/
    parasite-is-the-first-sexual-critique-of-capitalism/

7   Walter Benjamin, "Capitalism as Religion" from Walter
    Benjamin, *Selected Writings Volume One*, trans. Rodney
    Livingstone (Havard: Harvard University Pressn1921, 1996)
    pp. 288–291. Available online at: https://cominsitu.wordpress.
    com/2018/06/08/capitalism-as-religion-benjamin-1921/

CHAPTER THREE: THE SOCIAL FUNCTION OF THE MONSTER THROUGH THE AGES

1   See: Jeffrey Cohen, "Monster Culture: Seven Theses," in *Monster
    Theory: Reading Culture*, ed. Jeffrey Cohen, (Minnesota: University
    of Minnesota Press, 1996).

2   Edmund Burke, *Reflections on the Revolution in France*, ed. Frank
      Turner (New Haven, CT: Yale University Press, 2003), p. 179.
      Emphasis my own.

3   Mary Shelley, *Frankenstein* (London: Penguin Books, 2012), p 119.

4   C. L. R. James, *The Black Jacobins, Toussaint L'Ouverture and the
      Haitian Revolution* (London: Vintage Books, 1989), pp. 24–25.

5   Quoted in: Marie Mulvey-Roberts, *Dangerous Bodies: Historicising
      The Gothic Corporeal* (Manchester: Manchester University Press,
      2016), p. 56.

6   Ibid., p. 57.

7   See: Lee Sterrenberg, "Mary Shelley's Monster: Politics and
      Psyche in Frankenstein" in *The Endurance of Frankenstein, Essays on
      Mary Shelley's Novel*, ed. George Levine and U.C. Knopflemacher
      (Berkley: University of California Press, 1979), p. 143.

8   Shelley, p. 47.

9   Shelley, p. 120

10   See Chris Baldick, *In Frankenstein's Shadow: Myth Monstrosity and
      Nineteenth Century Writing* (Oxford: Clarendon Press 1989).

11   Franco Moretti, "The Dialectic of Fear," *New Left Review*, 136
      (1982). Available online at: http://knarf.english.upenn.edu/
      Articles/moretti.html

12   Eric Hobsbawm, *The Age of Revolution 1749–1848* (London:
      Vintage Books, 1996), pp. 111–112.

13   Joshua Clover, *Riot Strike Riot: The New Era of Uprisings* (London:
      Verso Books, 2016).

14   For an explanation of the Blochian Not-Yet, see: Wayne Hudson,
      The Marxist Philosophy of Ernst Bloch (London: Palgrave, 1982).

15   E. P. Thompson, *The Making of the English Working Class* (London:
      Vintage Books, 1966).

16   Vladimir Lenin, *Imperialism: The Highest Stage of Capitalism*,
      available online at: https://www.marxists.org/archive/lenin/

works/1916/imp-hsc/. See also: Friedrich Engels, *The Condition of the Working Class In England* (Oxford: Oxford World Classics, 2009).

17 Bram Stoker, *Dracula* (London: Penguin Classics, 2003), p. 29.

18 Moretti, p. 73.

19 Karl Marx, *The Economic and Philosophic Manuscripts of 1844* (Moscow: Progress Publishers, 1959). Available online and translated by Martin Milligan at Marxists.org. https://www.marxists.org/archive/marx/works/1844/manuscripts/preface.htm

20 Steve Shaviro, "Capitalist Monsters," *Historical Materialism*, 10(4) (2002), p. 285.

21 Katie Stone, "Hungry for Utopia, An Anti-Work Reading of Bram Stoker's *Dracula*," *Utopian Studies*, 32(2) (2021), pp. 296–310.

22 Stoker, p. 60.

23 Stone, p. 306.

24 Stoker, p. 300.

25 Stone, p. 307.

26 Karl Marx, *Capital*, Volume One, Chapter Ten. Available online at: https://www.marxists.org/archive/marx/works/1867-c1/ch10.htm. My emphasis added.

27 Karl Marx, *The Economic and Philosophic Manuscripts 1844,* (Moscow: Progress Publishers 1959). Available online and translated by Martin Milligan at Marxists.org. https://www.marxists.org/archive/marx/works/1844/manuscripts/preface.htm

28 Paul Lafargue, *The Right to Be Lazy and Other Studies,* (London: Charles Kerr & Co 1883). Available online at: https://www.marxists.org/archive/lafargue/1883/lazy/ch02.htm.

CHAPTER FOUR: IT'S IN THE BLOOD

1   Xavier Aldana Reyes, "Body Horror," in *The Cambridge Companion to American Horror*, ed. Steven Shapiro and Mark Storey (Cambridge: Cambridge University Press, 2022), p. 118.

2   For more on this, see Stiegler's three-volume work *Technics and Time* that appeared in English between 1998 to 2010 (California, Stanford University Press)

3   Walter Benjamin, *The Arcades Project*, trans. Howard Eiland and Kevin McLaughlin (Harvard: Harvard University Press, 1999), p. 473.

4   For more on the role of debt, see: Maurizio Lazzarato, *The Making of the Indebted Man: An Essay on the Neoliberal Condition*, trans. John Ebert (Cambridge: MIT Press, 2011). For the link between human capital and resilience, see: David Chandler and Julian Reid, *The Neoliberal Subject: Resilience, Adaptation and Vulnerability* (London: RLI, 2016).

5   Again, for more on the political economy of this microwork, see: Phil Jones, *Work without the Worker: Labour in the Age of Platform Capitalism* (London: Verso Books, 2021).

CHAPTER FIVE: WITCHES, AND BEING A MONSTER TO CAPITALISM

1   Jenni Fink, "Catholic Exorcist Holding Special Mass to Counter Witches' Hex on Kavanaugh," *Newsweek* (October 18, 2018), available online at: https://www.newsweek.com/catholic-exorcist-holding-special-mass-counter-witches-hex-kavanaugh-1176666

2   Jude Doyle, "How Capitalism Turned Woman Into Witches," *In These Times* (January 31, 2019), available online at: https://

inthesetimes.com/article/capitalism-witches-women-witch-hunting-sylvia-federici-caliban

3 See: Taylor Swift, "I Did Something Bad", lyrics available at: http://www.genius.com/Taylor-Swift-i-did-something-bad-lyrics.

4 Madeline Miller, "From Circe to Clinton: Why powerful women are cast as witches," *The Guardian* (April 7, 2018), available online at: https://www.theguardian.com/books/2018/apr/07/cursed-from-circe-to-clinton-why-women-are-cast-as-witches

5 Sourcing this quote is easier said than done, but the best evidence of the internet suggests this novel, an alternative history of the Salem witch trials, as its source. See Tish Thawer, *The Witches of Blackbrook* (London: Amber Leaf Publishing 2015)

6 See: Elizabeth Parker, *The Forest and The Eco-Gothic: The Deep Dark Woods in the Popular Imagination* (London: Palgrave Macmillan, 2020), particularly pp. 181–184.

7 Nathaniel Hawthorne, *Young Goodman Brown and Other Tales* (Oxford: Oxford University Press, 2009). pp. 111–124

8 Sylvia Federici, *Caliban and the Witch: Women: The Body and Primitive Accumulation* (London: Autonomedia Books, 2004). While Federici's historiography has come in for substantial criticism, the *mode* of analysis put forward in the book remains highly compelling, especially in conjunction with her earlier work around wages for housework.

9 Jonathan Greenaway, *Theology, Horror and Fiction: A Reading of the Gothic Nineteenth Century* (London: Bloomsbury Academic Press, 2020).

10 Alexander Howard and Julian Murphet, "Transferring Suspiria: Historicism and Philosophies of Psychoanalytic Transference," *Film-Philosophy* (Feb 2022), pp. 63–85, available online at: https://www.euppublishing.com/doi/full/10.3366/film.2022.0190

11   Ulrike Meinhof, *Everybody Talks about The Weather... We Don't — The Collected Writings of Ulrike Meinhof* (London: Seven Stories Press, 2008), p. 138.

12   Alexander Howard and Julian Murphet, "Transferring *Suspiria:* Historicism and Philosophies of Psychoanalytic Transference" in *Film-Philosophy* Vol 26.1 pp 63–85. Full text available online.

13   Ernst Bloch, *The Principle of Hope*, Volume One, trans. Neville Plaice, Stephen Plaice, and Paul Knight (Cambridge: MIT Press 1995), p. 398.

14   Comprising films that (as an online meme puts it) celebrate both women's rights and women's wrongs. The "Good for her" film is a film in which a female protagonist's actions are seen as praiseworthy. Ari Aster's *Midsommar* (2019) is a paradigmatic example, wherein the main character burns her boyfriend to death and joins a newfound family/cult. The "Good for her" response can thus be seen as part of the liberal capitalist co-option of the witch, turning Suzy into a dancing girl boss instead of seeing her as an anti-fascist intervention into history. Bethany Squires's piece at *Vulture* offers a good, tongue-in-cheek overview: https://www.vulture.com/2023/03/an-attempt-to-define-the-good-for-her-cinematic-universe.html

15   The entire text is available to read online, thanks to the work of the Kafka Project: http://www.kafka.org/index.php?aid=161

16   Paul B. Preciado, *Can the Monster Speak?*, trans. Frank B. Wynne (London: Fitzcarraldo Editions, 2020), pp. 28–29.

17   Preciado, p. 35.

18   Preciado, p. 41.

19   Read the whole series of aphorisms here: https://happyhourathippels.wordpress.com/2022/07/15/preliminary-theses-on-gothic-communism-monstrous-excess-and-the-eschaton/.

20   Preciado, p. 70.

21 For an exploration of the "Not-Yet" in the work of Ernst Bloch, see: Wayne C. Hudson, *The Marxist Philosophy of Ernst Bloch* (London: Palgrave Macmillan, 1988).

22 Judith Butler, "Why is the idea of gender provoking backlash the world over?" *The Guardian*, (October 23, 2021), available online at: https://www.theguardian.com/us-news/commentisfree/2021/oct/23/judith-butler-gender-ideology-backlash

23 Tom Moylan, *Becoming Utopian: The Culture and Politics of Radical Transformation* (London: Bloomsbury Academic, 2021).

24 Preciado, p. 75.

CHAPTER SIX: GHOSTS AND THE HAUNTING OF MODERNITY

1 James Bridle, *New Dark Age: Technology and the End of the Future* (London: Verso Books, 2018).

2 You can read the full short story on the digital H. P. Lovecraft archives: https://www.hplovecraft.com/writings/texts/fiction/cc.aspx

3 Wendy Liu, *Abolish Silicon Valley, How to Liberate Technology from Capitalism* (London: Repeater Books 2020).

4 Although, happily, not impossible: https://www.gmb.org.uk/uber/join

5 See Mark Fisher's work. The talk "All of this is temporary" is a great introduction to Fisher's concept of capitalist deflation: https://www.youtube.com/watch?v=deZgzw0YHQI

6 For a good overview of the development of the internet and the enclosure of the digital commons that was baked into the technology from its very beginnings, see: Ben Tarnoff, *Internet for the People, Fight for Our Digital Future* (London: Verso Books, 2022).

7 Timur Bekmambetov, "Beyond Unfriended: Timur Bekmambetov's wild plan to make desktop movies mainstream," interview with Bryan Bishop, *The Verge* (April 30, 2015), available

online at: https://www.theverge.com/2015/4/30/8514795/unfriended-timur-bekmambetov-desktop-movie-genre

8   Shane Denson and Julia Leyda, ed., *Post Cinema: Theorising 21st Century Film* (Falmer: REFRAME Books, 2016).

9   I'm indebted to the excellent podcast Wyrd Signal, which pointed out the important distinction between the mirror and cyberspace — listen to Wyrd Signal here: https://soundcloud.com/wyrdsignalpodcast. For perhaps the most essential recuperation and rethinking of millennial narcissism, see: Matt Colquhoun, *Narcissus in Bloom: An Alternative History of the Selfie* (London: Repeater Books, 2023).

10   Kiyoshi Kurosawa, "Interview with Kiyoshi Kurosawa," interview by Paul Matthews, *Reverse Shot*, (October 20, 2005), available online at: https://www.reverseshot.org/interviews/entry/1503/kiyoshi-kurosawa

11   See: https://harpers.org/archive/2008/09/on-the-economy-of-the-dead/

12   Jing Yang, "Media Evolution, 'Double Edged Sword': Technology and Active Spectatorship: Investigating Desktop Film from Media Ecology Perspectives" in *PPGCOM – UFJF*, 14(1) (January 2020), p. 136.

13   Patrick Klepek, "Meet the teenager who says he's a swatter," *Kotaku* (February 17, 2015), available online at: https://web.archive.org/web/20230425043101/https://kotaku.com/meet-a-teenager-who-says-hes-a-swatter-1686128721

14   Nolen Gertz, *Nihilism and Technology* (London: Rowman & Littlefield, 2018), p. 192.

15   Of course, it should be pointed out that vast swathes of people — the poor and working classes — were not given the option of working from home, being euphemistically classed as "essential" — yet they were never essential enough to be paid properly or protected in the workplace.

16   See: https://www.theguardian.com/technology/2021/mar/01/
     zoom-revenues-results-coronavirus

17   Adam Kotsko, "What Happened to Giorgio Agamben?" *Slate*,
     (February 20, 2022), available online at: https://slate.com/
     human-interest/2022/02/giorgio-agamben-covid-holocaust-
     comparison-right-wing-protest.html

18   Franco Berardi, *The Third Unconscious* (London: Verso Books,
     2021), pp. 23–25.

19   Berardi, p. 34.

CHAPTER SEVEN: CRISES OF LIBERALISM AND NECRO-NEOLIBERALISM

1   *Saw X* (yes, really) was released on Halloween 2023 and has gone
     on to be the most critically well-regarded of the entire franchise.
     This means that Halloween 2024 will almost certainly see yet
     another instalment.

2   Achille Mbembe, "Necropolitics," trans. Libby Mentjes, *Public
     Culture*, 15(1) (Winter, 2003), pp. 11–40.

3   Carl Schmitt, *Political Theology Four Chapters on the Concept of
     Sovereignty,* trans. George Schwab (Chicago: University of Chicago
     Press, 2005), p. 5.

4   Mbembe, p. 13.

5   Which, for reasons of space and time, I won't be able to
     address here.

6   Mike David, *City of Quartz* (London: Verso Books, 2006).

7   See: Stacey Abbott, "When the Subtext Becomes Text: *The Purge*
     Takes on the American Nightmare," in *Horror Franchise Cinema*, ed.
     Mark McKenna (London: Routledge, 2022), pp. 128–142.

8   Malcolm X, "Speech At The Founding Rally for the
     Organisation for Afro-American Unity," available online at:
     https://www.blackpast.org/african-american-history/speeches-

african-american-history/1964-malcolm-x-s-speech-founding-rally-organization-afro-american-unity/

9   Fredric Jameson, *An American Utopia: Dual Power and the Universal Army* (London: Verso Books, 2016), p. 10.

10   Ibid., p. 11.

11   Vladimir Lenin, "The Dual Power," taken from *Lenin's Collected Works Vol. 24* (Moscow: Progress Publishers, 1964) pp 38–41. Available to read in full here: https://www.marxists.org/archive/lenin/works/1917/apr/09.htm

12   See: Marcello Tari, *There Is No Unhappy Revolution: The Communism of Destitution* (Philadelphia: Common Nations Press, 2021).

13   Matt Zoller Seitz, "*The Forever Purge,*" *Roger Ebert* (July 2, 2021), available online at: https://www.rogerebert.com/reviews/the-forever-purge-movie-review-2021

CHAPTER EIGHT: GOTHIC HISTORIOGRAPHY AND THE IDEA OF A (MONSTROUS) UTOPIA

1   See the classic work that is now sadly little read: Victor Sage, *Horror Fiction in the Protestant Tradition* (London: Palgrave Macmillan, 1988). One might flip Sage's argument on its head — perhaps we exist within a fantasy about history, and the so-called fantasy of the Gothic is a more honest and realistic vision of history…

2   Ernst Bloch, "Non-Synchronism and Its Obligation to Its Dialectics," *New German Critique*, 11 (Spring 1977), p. 22. This essay was originally written in 1932 and then later incorporated into the 1935 edition of Bloch's book *Heritage of Our Time*.

3   Ernst Bloch, *Heritage of Our Time*, trans. Neville and Stephen Plaice (London: Polity Press, 1991), p. 100.

4   Richard Gilman-Opalsky, *Spectres of Revolt: On the Intellect of Insurrection and Philosophy From Below* (London: Repeater Books, 2016).

5   Whereas Bloch was the great utopian, hopeful philosopher, Benjamin is far more pessimistic, but they both share a commitment to the romantic critique of capitalism and a heterodox though committed Marxism. See Michael Löwy, *Fire Alarm: Reading Walter Benjamin's "On The Concept of History"* (London: Verso Books, 1996).

6   Karl Marx, *The Eighteenth Brumaire of Louis Bonaparte* (1852), available online at: https://www.marxists.org/archive/marx/works/1852/18th-brumaire/ch01.htm.

7   China Mieville, "Fantasy and Revolution: An Interview With China Mieville," interview by John Newsinger, *International Socialism*, 2(88) (Autumn 2000), available online at: https://www.marxists.org/history/etol/writers/newsinger/2000/xx/mieville.htm

8   Fredric Jameson, *Postmodernism: The Cultural Logic of Late Capitalism* (London: Verso Books, 1992), p. 87.

9   See: China Mieville, *A Spectre, Haunting: On The Communist Manifesto* (London: Head of Zeus, 2023), pp. 140–181.

10 Thomas Ligotti, *My Work Is Not Yet Done: Three Tales of Corporate Horror* (London: Virgin Books, 2009).

11 Fredric Jameson, *Marxism and Form* (Princeton: Princeton University Press 1974), p.120.

12 Ibid., p. 128.

13 This is what Russell Jacoby refers to as the difference between the program utopians and the iconoclasts. See: Russell Jacoby, *Picture Imperfect: Utopian Thought for an Anti-Utopian Age* (New York: Columbia University Press, 2005).

14 China Mieville, "The Limits of Utopia," *Climate and Capitalism* (March 2, 2018), available online at: https://climateandcapitalism.com/2018/03/02/china-mieville-the-limits-of-utopia/

15 Ibid.

16 Again, see the productive set of aphorisms Adam posted at https://happyhourathippels.wordpress.com/ 2022/07/15/preliminary-theses-on-gothic-communism-monstrous-excess-and-the-eschaton/

17 Evan Calder Williams, *Combined and Uneven Apocalypse* (London: Zer0 Books, 2011), p. 8.

18 Ibid., p. 9.

CONCLUSION: WE'RE ALL MONSTERS NOW

1 For a good history of the monsters in antiquity, see: Stephen K. Asma, *On Monsters: An Unnatural History of Our Worst Fears* (Oxford: Oxford University Press, 2011).

2 An inarguable example of the way memes articulate truth in some form.

3 Alison Rumfitt, *Tell Me I'm Worthless* (Brighton: Cipher Press, 2021), pp. 232–233.

4 Ibid., p. 252.

5 Ernst Bloch, *The Principle of Hope*, vol 2, trans. Neville Plaice, Stephen Plaice, and Paul Knight (Harvard: MIT Press, 1995), p. 623.

6 Gretchen Felker-Martin, "Gretchen Felker-Martin's Manhunt is a new kind of horror novel," interview by Sarah Neilson, *Shondaland*, (February 22, 2022), available online at https://www.shondaland.com/inspire/books/a39141937/gretchen-felker-martins-manhunt/

7 Gretchen Felker-Martin, *Manhunt* (New York: Tor Book 2022), p. 25.

8 Paul Preciado, *Can The Monster Speak?* trans Frank B Wynne (London: Fitzcarraldo Editions 2020).

9 Felker-Martin, p. 111.

10 Ibid.

11   Gretchen Felker-Martin, "Gretchen Felker-Martin's *Manhunt* is more human than its critics," interview by Jordan Darville, *The Fader* (April 29, 2022), available online at: https://www.thefader.com/2022/04/29/gretchen-felcker-martin-manhunt-interview

12   Miéville (2022), p 184.

Acknowledgements

I am profoundly grateful to Tariq Goddard and the entire team at Repeater Books for their help, encouragement, and support for this book project, and to Carl Neville for his scrupulous editing and encouragement to be ambitious, rigorous and — where needed — polemical.

Much of this book was first worked out in conversation on a network of podcasts made up of working-class intellectuals and para-academics, so I must thank the entire *Acid Horizon* collective, as well as the hosts and listeners of *Revolutionary Left Radio*, *The Regrettable Century*, *Death Sentence*, *The Left Page*, and — of course — *Horror Vanguard*.

My most sincere thanks to China Miéville, Margaret Cohen, David McNally, and Mark Steven for casting unique profane illuminations onto the term "Gothic Marxism" in all their various ways. For that, I have nothing but the deepest comradely appreciation. I also greatly appreciate Mark Steven offering notes and feedback on the entire manuscript.

To Ash and Kyle, my dearest friends, thank you, thank you, thank you. Here's to many more books between us.

Finally, and above all of them, to my wife, Emma, the most brilliant writer and thinker I know, who has believed in this book even when I did not. It is to her that all my writing is dedicated, for without her none of it would exist.

REPEATER BOOKS

is dedicated to the creation of a new reality. The landscape of twenty-first-century arts and letters is faded and inert, riven by fashionable cynicism, egotistical self-reference and a nostalgia for the recent past. Repeater intends to add its voice to those movements that wish to enter history and assert control over its currents, gathering together scattered and isolated voices with those who have already called for an escape from Capitalist Realism. Our desire is to publish in every sphere and genre, combining vigorous dissent and a pragmatic willingness to succeed where messianic abstraction and quiescent co-option have stalled: abstention is not an option: we are alive and we don't agree.